KB077182

Succeeding as a Retiree :
How to Prepare for Your Second Career

Succeeding as a retiree : How to Prepare for Your Second Career

Publication Date | January 24, 2024
Author | Kim Kwan-youl(김관열)
Publisher | Han Geon-hee(한건희)
Published by | Bookk Co., Ltd.
Publisher's Registration | July 15, 2014 (No. 2014-16)
Address | 305 A-dong, SK Twin Towers, 119 Gasan Digital
          1-ro, Geumcheon-gu, Seoul, South Korea
Phone | 1670-8316
Email | info@bookk.co.kr

ISBN | 979-11-410-6865-3

Title:

Succeeding as a retiree:
How to Prepare for Your Second Career

Author: Kim Kwan-youl

BOOKK

[Starting Off]

To all the retirees preparing for their second careers, this book is dedicated.

One day, a soon-to-be retiree visited me with growing fear as the retirement age approached. After reading my first book, 'Eun-jun-in' (meaning 'people preparing for retirement' in Korean), he sought me out for further guidance. What started as a brief conversation turned into a two-day journey. The joy he expressed upon finding the answers he had been seeking was immense. This experience filled me with gratitude. He goes by the name Visitor, and I am Mentor. If the conversations between Visitor and Mentor over those two days can shape the second act of one's life, what could be more extraordinary? While it may not provide the ultimate answer, I believe it is the right path to find one. I wish to serve as living proof. Allow me to present 'Success as a Retiree: How to Prepare for Your Second Career'. Now, let the conversation unfold. Retirement will no longer be a source of fear.

「Table of Contents」

Starting Off

9. Growing Happiness with age

1

Unexpected Visit

The visitor arrived at a slightly shabby three-story building nestled in a bustling food alley. The cozy pop-up bar occupied the first floor, while a vintage-style pub adorned the second floor. As he ascended through the garage door, he encountered an entrance embellished with a plaque that read 'ARTSPACE19.' With a quick phone call, a middle-aged gentleman appeared, introducing himself as the director of the 'Retirement Preparation Practical Research Institute' and handing over his business card. The visitor followed him into an office that resembled the living room of a typical home. One side was occupied by a refrigerator, microwave, and water purifier, while a PC on a table showcased ongoing work on the other side. A bookshelf filled with books of various titles stood in a corner, and two dining tables occupied the center of the room. In front of the sink, there was a table displaying an assortment of condiments. Though not impeccably organized, the atmosphere radiated a sense of familiarity, as if one could accomplish everything in one place. Despite feeling exhausted from an early morning drive, the visitor was filled with anticipation and excitement, knowing that they had come here to find something important. After taking a moment to catch their breath, the visitor slowly began to speak.

A strange hideout by the name of 'ARTSPACE19'

Visitor : Thank you for welcoming me sincerely. I noticed the sign

'ARTSPACE19' on the entrance door and I understand that this place is intended to be used as an art space. However, it doesn't give me the feeling of being in an art space.

Mentor: 'ARTSPACE19' doesn't mean it's an art space. The abbreviation ART stands for 'After Retirement'. So, 'ARTSPACE19' means my own space after retirement. The number 19 means that I started my retirement in 2019.

Visitor : I see. That's very interesting. When you were introduced on the broadcast as ART coach, did it mean in the same sense?

Mentor: Indeed, that is correct. Simply put, an 'Art Coach' is a coaching expert who assists retirees in preparing well for their post-retirement life.

After hearing an explanation of the title from him, the visitor suddenly felt that it was more systematic than he had thought. He began to feel a sense of great anticipation. He started to have hope that he could find answers on how to prepare for the second act of his life after retirement.

Visitor : So, it seems like this space is very special to you. What does ARTSPACE19 mean to you?

Mentor: ARTSPACE19 is a very important place to me. It can be said that the first task that retirees should prepare for a successful post-retirement life is to secure a commuting space like this.

Visitor : The first task? Is it that important? If we have a spare room at home, can't we use it? It can save costs.

Mentor: However, it will be subject to many restrictions. If you just stay at home after retirement, you won't be able to sustain a successful retirement life for long. Moreover, your wife won't like it. Even if the couple is close, if they spend all day together after retirement, it is obvious that it will be a big cause to create new trouble between them.

Visitor : Ah! That could be possible. I agree with the need for a commuting space. So, what do you do here?

Mentor: It's a place to live a new life in the true act two of my life. I call this place 'the base camp' where all retirees can design and implement act two of their lives that they have dreamed of. I will have the opportunity to explain this in more detail later.

Visitor : I understand. But I haven't introduced myself yet. I am a retiree-to-be who has two years left until retirement. I have worked for the company for over 30 years. I was worried about what to prepare when I retire, so I came to see you after hearing that you are the best expert in this field. Thank you for welcoming me.

Mentor: The best expert? No, not really. Anyway, thank you for coming from far away. What were you most curious about?

Visitor : Before coming here, I looked at your profile through a media article. You seem to have produced many results in various fields. You wrote a book titled 'Eun-jun-in' which means the people who are preparing for retirement. I was curious about what it means.

Mentor: The Korean title, Eun-jun-in is translated into English as 'Retirement planners', which means people who are preparing for retirement. And it is a neologism that I created. It is a term that contrasts with 'chui-jun-saeng', which means job seekers. As you know, 'chui-jun-saeng' is a word that refers to students who are preparing for employment and has now become a new word that is included in our Korean dictionary. We can easily divide our lives into three stages. I express that as the 'Trifle 30' era. It means that 30 years can be divided into three stages. If we describe these three stages in simple terms, the first stage can be called the preparation stage for independence, the second stage can be called the economic activity stage, and the third stage can be called the retirement stage. Through a lot of preparation, we become job seekers in the first stage for the second stage of the economic activity period. Starting from elementary school, through middle school, high school, and college, we prepare a lot to become good job seekers, don't we? Do you know what the necessary conditions for good job seekers are these days in Korea?

Visitor : The requirements for good job seekers? Grades? Foreign language skills? I'm not quite sure.

Mentor: It is said that nowadays, at least 9 conditions are necessary to become a good job seeker in Korea. When I graduated from college and started looking for jobs in the past, we only needed about three things, such as the university title, grades, and our English scores, and it wasn't very difficult to get a job. But nowadays, it is said that there are six more things needed in addition to those three. These include overseas training experience, volunteering experience, various certifications, contest awards, and internship experience. Recently, there is one more thing that is needed, and that is plastic surgery. However, even with all these preparations, getting a job is not easy. Anyway, we prepare so much for the success of the second stage of life, but I don't know what you have prepared specifically for the last 30 years of the third stage of life, which is called the golden age of life. It seems that most people just face the third stage without specific preparations during the second stage. So, retirement can be very scary to us as we face it without any special preparation.

Visitor : I see. I can totally relate. There must be a reason why retirement is so scary.

Why do retirees fear retirement?

Mentor: That's right. According to a survey by one of the portal sites, when examining why people who are about to retire are afraid of retirement, the second reason is the loss of a fixed source of income, the third reason is having children who still need financial support, the fourth reason is that life after retirement is too long, and the fifth reason is a decrease in self-esteem. Can you guess what the first reason is?

Visitor : Hmm, I'm not sure."

Mentor: The first reason why people are afraid of retirement is because they haven't properly prepared for retirement yet. A whopping 65.1% of all participants agreed with this reason, which is even higher than the combined percentage of reasons 2 through 5. Therefore, the important thing is to prepare for retirement well, and only then will the fear of retirement disappear. In other words, just like a university student job seekers, retirees also need to prepare for something specific. Let's become 'Eun-jun-in' who prepares for retirement well in the second stage of life for the third stage of life.

5 reasons why retirement is scary

1 Unprepar- edness	2 Loss of income	3 Dependent children	4 Longevity	5 Decreased self-esteem

Visitor : It's really interesting. There's a profound meaning behind the term 'Eun-jun-in'. So, how did you come to write the book?"

The birth of a retirement preparation guidebook

Mentor: Writing a book was not my intention from the beginning. I spent 35 years very busy in a public enterprise. By government policy, the retirement age was extended from 58 to 60 years old. Suddenly, two more years were added.

Since I was excluded from the approval line, I had spare time and I utilized it to read many books in various fields. Then, as my retirement date approached, I felt like I should prepare for retirement and started looking for books related to retirement. I searched and found about 40 related books on the internet. So I chose all the books I could get and bought about 20 books and read them. I admit that they were all good books, but the problem was that I couldn't find a book that provided specific practical guidelines on what and how ordinary retirees like me should prepare for retirement. Even though I participated in the retirement preparation program provided by the company and met with some experts or retired seniors, I couldn't get specific answers.

Visitor : I see. So what did you do about it?

Mentor: I realized that there was no practical guidebook on how to prepare for retirement in Korea, so I decided to create one myself. I spent about two years developing basic theories and practical tools, and included my own experiences in the book, which became the retirement preparation guidebook 'Eun-jun-in'.

Visitor : Oh, I see. So that's how the book titled 'Eun-jun-in' was born. It must be easy for anyone to follow since it's a practical guidebook based on your two-year experience. So, what are the basic concepts included in 'Eun-jun-in'?

Mentor: The principle is very simple. My goal in life after retirement is to have a dignified life. In order to have a dignified life, specific preparation is necessary. It is the key to success or failure in retirement life how specifically you prepare for it. Therefore, I thought that I needed to know what to prepare for in each area of life in order to make specific preparations. So, in order to find those areas, I first imagined various scenarios for our life after retirement and tried to categorize them. As a result, I realized that if I divided them into at least four areas, everything would be covered.

Visitor : Four areas of life?

Mentor: Yes, there are four areas. I thought that if I divided them into these four areas, everything would be covered.

Visitor : So what are these four areas of life?

Mentor: This is really important. There are four areas of life: the first is living well independently, the second is living well with others, the third is the area of constant self-challenge, and the last is the area of serving others. When abbreviated into one word for each area, they form **Sollive** (solo + live) for living well independently, **Comlive** (community + live) for living well with others, **Challive** (challenge + live) for the area of constant self-challenge, and **Vollive** (volunteering + live) for the area of serving others.

4 areas of retirement preparation

Sollive	Comlive
Challive	Vollive

Visitor : So, you're saying that the four areas of life are Sollive, Comlive, Challive, and Vollive? The words are very interesting. So, if we prepare well for these four areas of life, are you saying we can be well prepared for retirement?

What are the 4 areas of retirement preparation?

Mentor: So, to summarize, to have a successful retirement, one must prepare specifically for each of these four areas, just like a student preparing for a job. However, I feel that many people do not prepare specifically for any of these four areas. Therefore, I believe that if you prepare specifically for these four areas of life, you can have almost perfect retirement preparation. However, you may feel that there is something missing, about 2%.

Visitor : You mentioned that we can have almost perfect retirement preparation if we prepare specifically for each of these four areas of life. However, there is still a missing 2%, what does that mean?

Mentor: In a way, this can be considered a highlight of my book 'Eun-jun-in'. It is about connecting this preparation to one's future career. It's about finding what really fits and what one wants to do in the future. In other words, it's about finding one's own future self-brand during the retirement preparation process. I named this the **'Self-core brand,'** which is more about creating something new than just finding it.

Visitor : So ultimately, your point is that we should create our own self-core brand as the direction we should go. Is that correct?

Self-core brand! Anyone can create it.

Mentor: That's right. Self-core brand! It's not a difficult term. In short, during the retirement preparation process in four areas, if each person discovers and specializes in the field they are interested in, and commercializes it, that can become their self-core brand. Later, it can even develop into their second career in the future. In essence, searching for a job for a short-term reemployment or starting a new business after retirement differs significantly from creating a self-core brand

Creation of Self-core brand

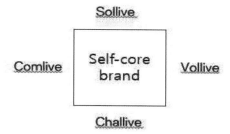

Visitor : Did you say that searching for short-term reemployment or starting a new business after retirement is fundamentally different from creating a self-core brand?

Mentor: That's right. If we want to live a better life after retirement, we need to have a balanced life in the four areas of our lives and develop our self-core brand. This is precisely the core of my book 'Eun-jun-in' - creating the '4 areas of Retirement Preparation' and 'Self-core brand'.

Visitor : Then, how can you prove that we can successfully prepare for retirement using that method?

Mentor: I can confidently prove this. Embarrassingly enough, I am the good example of this. Although it has only been a few years since I retired, no one knew that I would become a professional writer in the field of retirement, a professional lecturer in various fields, and even a lyricist who would release music albums. Not only that, I also play instruments such as drums and shoulder keyboards, make steaks and bread, and even enjoy sewing as a hobby, living an interesting life that no one knew about. These were things that I myself could not have predicted.

Visitor : You also lecture in various fields?

Mentor: At first, based on my book 'Eun-jun-in', I lectured on retirement preparation. It was really fun. I realized that lecturing was something that suited me. I decided to try lecturing in other fields. So, in addition to retirement preparation, I give lectures in various fields such as safety, civil defense, happy senior life, and nuclear power P.A. etc.

Visitor : I searched on Naver and found out that you are active in many other fields besides this. Is that correct?

Mentor: You searched about me. That's correct. I am currently active as a YouTuber with more than 10,000 subscribers and 2 million views, and also as a certified job interview examiner for companies and a mentor for college students' job interviews. Recently, I also published a book of poems and took a step into the world of a poet. All of these can be traced back to my development of '4 areas of Retirement Preparation' and 'Self-core brand,' which I introduced in my book.. These challenges continue to evolve. Recently, as a writer, I have made efforts to specialize in the field of retirement preparation. As a result of these endeavors, I have published another book. The title of my second retirement-related book is 'Succeeding as a Baecksoo After Retirement'.

Visitor : Did you mention that you have published a second book related to retirement preparation? That's truly an impressive achievement.

Mentor: That's very kind of you to say. Becoming a specialized writer in retirement-related topics is my biggest goal. It can be considered as my primary self-core brand.

Visitor : So how many jobs do you have right now?

Mentor: I don't really like to call them jobs, but there are six things I'm doing because I enjoy them. My current titles are writer, lecturer, YouTuber, lyricist, interviewer, and job mentor. Although I don't earn a lot in each area, I make a little profit in each field through my effort.

Visitor: You really seem to be doing a lot even after retirement. I'm looking forward to hearing more from you.

The visitor didn't have many conversations with the mentor, but he had a feeling that there was something special hidden in this place. As he talked with him, he couldn't contain his excitement thinking about his future life. His voice trembled a little, unable to hide his exhilaration.

Visitor : It's truly impressive and remarkable that you have taken on the roles of a writer, instructor, YouTuber, lyricist, interviewer, and job mentor within a relatively short period since your retirement. However, before coming here, I had a question that I was curious about. What do you think is the biggest problem for retirees?

The biggest misconception about retirement

Mentor: As I mentioned, to enjoy retirement life, you need to prepare well for four areas of life - Sollive, Comlive, Challive, and Vollive. In other words, you need to prepare specific activities for each area in advance that are suitable for you. It's like a student preparing for a job, preparing something specific in the first stage of life for the second stage of their life.

Visitor : Yes, you said that. I totally agree with you.

Mentor: But you see, many retirees do not prepare specifically for any of these four areas. So many people usually think that they can prepare one by one when they have a lot of time after retirement. I think that is the biggest problem and misconception of retirees.

Visitor: So, are you saying that retirement preparation means preparing before retirement, rather than preparing after retirement?

Mentor: That's right. Preparing for retirement after end-of-term retirement is like a student who prepares for employment after graduating from college. You need to prepare in advance for the third phase of your life. However, the important thing is that you need to prepare more specifically. If someone has prepared each of the four areas of retirement preparation specifically, that person can be considered to have prepared well for retirement than anyone else. It may not be perfect, but if you continue to build on it, you can say that retirement preparation is progressing almost perfectly.

2

A life enjoyed alone

(Sollive)

Visitor : I think we need to look more closely at the four retirement preparation areas: Sollive, Comlive, Challive, and Vollive. Could you explain to me more easily what we need to prepare for in each of these areas?

Mentor: O.K! Ultimately, the first key to retirement preparation will be how to find activities that suit oneself in each of these four areas. I don't think this is a difficult approach.

Visitor : Then, could you give me an easy-to-understand example of how you would prepare for such things?

No Sollive, no second half of life

Mentor: That's right. Now is the important part. Just listen to me. First, you need to prepare for 'Sollive.' In other words, it means preparing for a life where you can enjoy yourself even after retirement. The preparation for Sollive can be considered the cornerstone of your retired life. After the end-of-term retirement, you will have to lead a completely different life than when you were working. If you are not prepared to enjoy yourself alone, your life after retirement will be very difficult. If you are not well-prepared for Sollive, your second life after retirement will be a complete disaster. In other words, after retirement, you cannot rely on the relationships you had with your colleagues or subordinates from your past job. You cannot rely on them, and you cannot expect them to continue. Although your relationship with your family, including your wife, may deepen to some extent compared to when you were working, you cannot rely on them completely. That's why you need to prioritize being well-prepared to enjoy yourself alone.

4 areas of retirement preparation

Solo +Live

Sollive	Comlive
Challive	Vollive

Visitor : So, what kind of specific preparation do I need to make for Sollive?

Mentor: To prepare for Sollive, it is important to prepare three main things. First, prepare a living space that you can go to after retirement. It means you need to prepare a place like a base camp where you can go to work every day.

Prepare your base camp for retirement

Visitor : Ah! ARTSPACE19! Are you talking about this place?

Mentor: That's right. After retirement, most retirees end up staying at home or going to places like city libraries. It's not so desirable. Imagine if a retiree stays at home all day after retirement. It will be truly terrible for their spouse. If you end up staying at home after retirement, have you ever imagined how much of a burden you would be for your wife who has been taking care of the household all these years?

Visitor : But after retirement, isn't it not easy to find a place to commute even if we try to find one?

Mentor: So, we need to prepare beforehand. Listen to this. In our country, 45% of wives feel annoyed by their retired husbands. What's even more surprising is that retirees spend an average of 4 hours and 10 minutes with their spouses, excluding sleeping time. Most women even want to reduce that time. After retirement, husbands want to relax at home, but the reality is not so. Do you know what three things men stare at when they are at home after retirement?

Visitor : TV, and what else?

Mentor: The three things that retired husbands usually stare at are TV, wife, and dogs. According to a survey by a research institute, 77.6% of retirees' leisure time is spent watching TV, while 8.7% is spent on household chores, 7.9% on talking with family, and only 3.2% is spent on hobbies with their spouses. It's not a good thing if they only watch TV at home after retirement. Therefore, preparing a space for commuting every day after retirement is more important than anything else.

Visitor: You're saying that even though someone retired, he still need a place to commute to in the morning. I completely understand and agree with you.

Mentor: Having a personal space to commute to every day after retirement is really important. This is something that needs to be prepared before entering retirement. The reason for this is because retirement is a different time from the past, and creating a new future while staying at home is difficult. This space is like a base camp, and it will be a multi-purpose room with five objectives. First, it will be a planning space for the future, second, a learning space, third, a space for hobbies, fourth, a resting space, and finally, it can also be used as a meeting space.

Visitor : However, wouldn't there be a financial problem in preparing this personal space for daily commuting?

Mentor: That's right. Of course, there may be financial concerns. Therefore, the second preparation for 'Sollive' is the need for some of the living expenses that can be used under self-management. I will explain this in more detail later, but various living expenses will be required even after retirement. However, the most important part of these living expenses should be considered from this. Of course, it doesn't have to be expensive or luxurious. If you take the time to search in advance, you will find that it is not as difficult as you think.

Visitor : The first item to prepare for 'Sollive', a life that can be enjoyed well alone, is to secure a living space for commuting after retirement. Then, what is the second item for 'Sollive'?

Mentor: The second item for 'Sollive' is to secure a fixed living expense that can be used under one's own management after retirement.

Retirement expenses are bullets in battle

Visitor : Are you seriously talking about the issue of money for after retirement?

Mentor: Yes, that's right. Actually, it's very difficult to talk about this issue of money because it is a sensitive topic. In fact, I think this is a very important part. According to my research, one of the biggest reasons why many retired seniors cannot lead a good retired life is because they did not prepare enough for this. Of course, there may be some parts that are difficult to judge because each household has its own style of managing finances or slightly different financial situations. However, I strongly emphasize that this is an area that you should pay particular attention to.

Visitor : But don't most retirees think they need to keep making money even after retirement for various economic reasons?

Mentor: Of course. If you can naturally find a job and earn money after retirement, you should do so. But such opportunities are rare. I have seen many retirees who are solely focused on making money again after retirement. However, I think it is much more important to focus on how to manage the money earned so far and the future pension. Therefore, taking each individual's situation into account, I highly recommend securing a monthly living expenses under one's own management after retirement. It's like having bullets to use on a battlefield.

Visitor : So, what specifically should one do to achieve this?

Mentor: Actually, even I did not know exactly how much my

expected income would be after retirement. But it is very clear that if this part is not well planned, it can act as an obstacle to many things one wants to do after retirement. It means that things like securing a personal living space can become difficult, making it difficult to have a systematic retirement life from the beginning. Therefore, you should clarify this part before retiring, and there are several things you need to do.

Visitor : You mentioned that there are some things that need to be done. What are they?"

Mentor: There are three things to consider. First, you should accurately understand your expected income sources after retirement. For example, there may be retirement pensions, national pensions, or personal pensions, as well as various other sources of income. For example, rental income from commercial properties or securities and funds. Although it may differ for each individual, you should accurately understand how much all of these income sources will generate annually after retirement.

Visitor : You mentioned that it's important to have an accurate understanding of each individual's expected income after retirement before anything else. What is the second thing to consider?"

Mentor: The second thing is to make a judgment on how to utilize the sources of income and tentatively determine the management entity for each source of income after consulting with the spouse. Thirdly, based on the agreed results between the couple, it is recommended to establish a guideline for personal expenditures. This way, you can systematically manage your living expenses on your own.

Visitor : Then, I'm curious to know how you proceeded with this.

Mentor: Of course, in my case, there was some disagreement with my wife, but we had enough discussion and were able to make a decision. In this case, never play games with your spouse, and it is recommended to consult thoroughly according to your own household situation and make a decision in advance before retirement. Although people tend to hush up about money issues, you must clearly recognize that it becomes the most important issue for retirees.

visitor : Did you not encounter any difficulties in the process?

Mentor: Yes, there were. In fact, the difference between my wife's thoughts and my thoughts was huge. I never expected it. So, we took the time to exchange our thoughts and reached a final consensus. It is a moment where trust in each other is somewhat necessary. If there had been no such consultation beforehand, I might have wandered around for a long time even after retirement. That's why I'm saying never to play games. It is more important to be honest about each other's positions.

Visitor : I will definitely remember the saying 'Never play games with your spouse' about this. So, as a preparation for Sollive, you advised to prepare a place where you can commute every day and fixed monthly living expenses. Then, is there anything else that is needed for preparing Sollive?

Mentor: Of course, you should have those. Actually, the two things I mentioned earlier are the most basic things. The key to Sollive preparation is to prepare specific activities that you can enjoy alone after retirement.

Visitor : The advice is to prepare activities that you can enjoy alone after retirement. Could you please be more specific about that?

Mentor: After retirement, we naturally have more time alone. However, when we actually retire, we don't know what to do. Therefore, if we don't prepare specifically for the many hours we spend alone, we often waste time wandering without any plan.

Visitor : So, what should we do to avoid wandering aimlessly after retirement?

Prepare activities to enjoy alone

Mentor: It's simple. Before retirement, it's important for each person to prepare activities in advance. Even if you try to prepare something after retirement, it can be very difficult. Therefore, it is recommended to prepare each item for enjoying alone carefully before retirement. Although you may think that you will have more time to prepare after retirement, many retirees can easily empathize with the fact that it is not easy to prepare when you actually try to do so.

Visitor : But it may not be easy to find enjoyable activities to do alone. So, what type of activities can we prepare?

Mento : Indeed, finding enjoyable activities to do alone may not be easy at first. I remember struggling to find even one activity myself. To make it easier, I suggest thinking of each task as a specific 'activity' that requires action. Let me share some tips for selecting these activities.

Visitor : Please go ahead.

Mentor: Approaching from three perspectives, it is believed that you can easily select a suitable Sollive activity for yourself. To briefly explain, the first is to find something that you can do well alone after retirement, or to carefully consider what you want to do well. In particular, it is very important to find something that you can do well. You should know that there may be many things that you can do well, even among the things you haven't tried so far.

Visitor : Your statement is that the first step is to find something that one can do well or wants to do well. So, what is the second step?

Mentor: The second step is to choose an activity that is preferably productive or can be shared with others.

Visitor : So, what's the third step?

Mentor: The third step is also very important. It is suggested that one should find a creative and challenging activity if possible. In summary, these three things can be summarized as follows: 1) Something one can do well or wants to do well, 2) Something productive and shareable, 3) Something creative and challenging. To meet these three criteria, you need to take enough time and prepare specifically for your activities before retirement. If you don't plan ahead and prepare, you may feel scared as retirement approaches. Moreover, if you start looking for activities once you've retired, you may not find a good activity that suits you and end up wasting time without any direction.

3 criteria for selecting Sollive activity

Can do well & want to do	Productive & shareable	Creative & challenging

Visitor : I totally agree. It's amazing how much attention to detail and consideration is needed even for preparing just one Sollive activity. I'm embarrassed that I used to think I could just wait until after retirement and figure out what to do then.

Mentor: According to my research, more than 80% of retirees cannot live an attractive life if they don't put their preparation into action within 2 years after retirement. You need to be prepared before retirement so that you can naturally connect and create the foundation to enjoy your life alone. The preparation for Sollive becomes the cornerstone for a better retirement life. If the foundation for Sollive is shaken, even if preparation is well done in other areas, self-esteem will crumble and life after retirement will become very difficult. Therefore, preparation for this part is very important.

Visitor : Then, above all, I would like to hear about how you prepared for retirement in each area in a short period of time. Can you tell me about it?

Mentor: Of course. As an expert who researches and presents practical methods for retirement preparation, I often introduce the content that I have actually experienced and pursued during my lectures. I cannot say that what I have done so far is the most ideal, but I am presenting the content I have pursued as a sample. Of course, other people can find activities that suit them.

Visitor : I'm really interested in your content.

Mentor: The first Sollive activity I chose was Western-style cooking. It was something I had always wanted to try during my career. I wanted to be able to cook delicious food for my family, so I chose that activity as my first enjoyment in retirement. The specific execution of the activity is crucial, and for Western-style cooking, I chose to learn at a cooking academy. Most of the students there were high school students who were studying to become professional chefs. It was difficult at first, but I completed the course and was the first among the students to obtain a national qualification in Western-style cooking. I continued to develop my skills and now I enjoy cooking for my family and friends.

What's the best food for home chefs?

Visitor : Wow! That sounds amazing. What kind of food are you good at making?

Mentor: My specialty is garlic steak. Everyone loves it. When I make this dish, my wife recognizes me as the best home chef. For me, Western-style cooking is the most satisfying item in Sollive activities. Here is a tip from me. For husbands who want to be loved by their wives or families, there is one dish they can excel at and be praised as the best chef. Do you know what that is?

Visitor : Did you say we can be praised as the best chef by excelling at just one dish? Please tell me what that is.

Mentor: That is the steak. With a little bit of learning, it is slightly more difficult than boiling ramen but easier than making soybean paste stew. If you make this steak occasionally at

home, you will be praised as the best home chef. I mean
it.

Visitor : I'd love to taste the steak you made. I bet it would be
delicious.

Mentor: Is that so? I'm planning on making garlic steak myself for
dinner tonight. It's also part of the lesson.

Visitor : Wow! Thank you. I'm really looking forward to it.

Mentor: Please have the steak for dinner and we will continue with
the lecture. As I mentioned earlier, we will prepare activities
one by one that are suitable for each person. I have
provided detailed explanations in my book 'Eun-jun-in', with
pictures. Initially, I prepared eight activities as items for
Sollive.

Prepare activities in advance with specifics

Visitor : You initially selected eight activities. What were they?

Mentor: As I mentioned earlier, in addition to Western-style cooking,
I selected eight activities to try after retirement, including
learning baking skills to make home bakery, playing the
accordion, obtaining POP and calligraphy certifications,
practicing Hanmun Seoye, learning traditional Korean music
song, and creating a balcony garden. These were the
things I really wanted to try after retirement, so I started

preparing for each activity bit by bit before I retired, using my spare time after work or on weekends.

Visitor : You selected eight activities to prepare for Sollive. Did they go well?

Mentor: I worked on each activity a little bit every day. Through this preparation process, I obtained four certifications in Western-style cooking, baking, children's cooking instruction, and calligraphy out of the total of 12 certifications I acquired after retirement.

Visitor : Wow, that's amazing that you obtained four certifications in the Sollive field out of the total of 12 certifications you acquired. It's really impressive. So now we need to move on to the second area. You mentioned that Comlive is about enjoying life together. Why do you think preparing for Comlive after retirement is important?

Mentor: That's an excellent question, but let's finish dinner first and then continue with Comlive. As I promised earlier, I will prepare garlic steak for you. You must be hungry, so please wait a little while. It won't take long.

He stood up from his seat and put on a white cooking apron before heading to the refrigerator. He opened the refrigerator door and took out various ingredients, neatly organizing them on the table one by one. First, he placed two beef chunks on the cutting board. He then applied olive oil and sprinkled salt to season the meat. The visitor nodded in approval, impressed by his every move, which already showed the professionalism of an expert. When asked why he didn't sprinkle pepper, he replied that the scent of pepper would be best preserved when sprinkled during the grilling process. He heated the pan and put the meat in it, adding crushed black pepper and a lump of butter, sliced garlic, and rosemary, continuously basting the meat with the sauce. The delightful scent of the steak was already filling the room. He covered the cooked meat with foil to let it rest while making the sauce. He quickly made the sauce by mixing soy sauce, sugar, and ketchup in a 1:2:3 ratio, adding minced garlic, salt, and pepper, and adjusting the water ratio. When he served the dish on a luxurious white plate with garnish, it was truly a masterpiece of garlic steak. The two men exclaimed "Wow! Wow!" as if in competition and quickly finished their plates.

3

Life enjoyed together
(Com live)

Visitor : The steak was really delicious. How can you be so good at cooking? There seems to be nothing you can't do. It was truly a memorable and wonderful meal. I don't think I'll forget it for a long time.

Mentor: That's too kind of you to say that. Steak is delicious no matter who makes it. Do you happen to know where the secret lies?

Visitor : Well, I'm not sure.

Mentor: The secret lies in butter. There's an American saying, 'Butter makes everything better.' I think meat and butter go together very well. Anyway, thank you for enjoying the meal. Now, let's continue. I will explain about 'Comlive. Comlive is the preparation for a life that can be enjoyed together after retirement. Of course, it is important to get along with people around you in normal times, but it is even more important to prepare for a life that can be enjoyed together after retirement. This is because retirement is the time when the framework of human relationships changes the most in life. The human relationships formed mainly with colleagues during their working years will completely change, and they will have to form a sense of belonging and relationship in a new framework of human relationships. Based on my research, it appears that during this time, it is absolutely necessary to establish human relationships completely anew, and it is a time that requires selection and concentration.

4 areas of retirement preparation

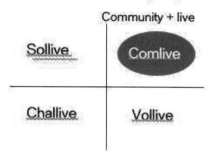

Community + live

Sollive	Comlive
Challive	Vollive

Visitor : Did you say 'selection and concentration'?

Mentor: Right. It's the time for selection and concentration. I've seen some people try various ways to form broader human relationships after retirement, but in some ways, it seems to be realistically luxurious and wasteful. This is because there are inevitably limitations and excessive money and time are invested in it. Therefore, I emphasize that you should proceed from the perspective of selection and concentration for forming new human relationships.

Visitor : I also strongly empathize with the statement that selection and concentration are necessary for forming new human relationships.

Comlive's selection and concentration

Mentor: That's correct. As I mentioned, it's about selection and concentration. Some people misunderstand what I'm saying and think that I'm suggesting intentionally breaking off relationships that have been formed so far. However, what I'm saying is not to be too attached to relationships that naturally come to an end and to accept it naturally.

Visitor : What criteria should be used for it?

Mentor: I would like to emphasize 3+1. Firstly, the three refer to friends, spouse, and family. It is important to create regular programs or events to spend time with these three groups. Of course, these programs may change or be discontinued over time, and new ones may be added, but it is important to develop a program that suits oneself from the beginning and consistently work on it for concrete retirement preparation.

3+1 focus groups for Comlive

Visitor : You mentioned 3 plus 1, but could you give an example of what the three refer to in your case? It would be easier to understand if you could introduce your case as an example.

Mentor: Sure, let me introduce my case. The three in 3+1 refer to friends, spouse, and family as I mentioned earlier.

Visitor : I see that friends, spouse, and family are the three in 3+1. What kind of programs have you prepared for them?

Mentor: I designed programs with a focus on sports mainly to achieve two goals: promoting health and building human relationships with my friends. After retirement, I wanted to challenge myself by trying new activities, such as playing three-cushion billiards, playing golf, learning shake-hand table tennis, and hiking in nearby areas. So, I created regular programs centered around these activities.

Visitor : You mentioned that the programs you have prepared for your friends are mainly sports programs, and among them, three-cushion billiards stands out.

Mentor: The sport that I wanted to learn the most while I was working was three-cushion billiards. When I was working abroad, I saw an elderly couple playing billiards and felt that it was a good exercise for seniors, which made me start learning it step by step after retirement. Although I'm still a beginner, I'm taking one step at a time towards my goal score (20 points).

Visitor : 3 cushion billiards is also a dream for many men. I sometimes watch it on TV and also feel like learning it once. However, I haven't thought about starting yet, but you put all your resolutions into practice. You are definitely a doer. By the way, billiards is indeed a great exercise for seniors.

Mentor: That's right, I also love golf and other sports such as table tennis, badminton, and bowling, but I think billiards is a really cool sport to play as you get older. I recommend it to everyone regardless of gender.

Visitor : Oh, I see. Then, did you prepare a separate program for your wife?

Mentor: Of course. It's a really important part. It wasn't easy to decide as I had to consider my wife's preferences. After discussing with my wife several times, I finally prepared two regular programs for her.

Visitor : Oh, this really makes me curious. What is it?

Mentor: The first one is a leisurely hike in Gyeongju Namsan

Mountain, and the second one is a regular mahjong game with my wife for preventing dementia. For my wife, who dislikes hiking, I named it 'slowpoke hiking' and it involves climbing various courses of Gyeongju Namsan Mountain regularly. As for the second mahjong game, I had the mahjong set at home for a long time, but I didn't have a mahjong board, so I made one myself and studied the rules. I explained it to my wife in an easy-to-understand way and we started playing. We started playing for preventing dementia, but nowadays we play for enjoying chicken and beer.

Visitor : Playing mahjong with your wife? That's quite unexpected.

Mentor: My wife is not yet good at it, but she is enjoying learning the game step by step. It's not much different from chess played in foreign countries. However, the rules can be a bit complex at first, so it takes some time to become proficient.

Visitor : Hiking slowly with your wife and playing mahjong together?

You must be enjoying your time with your wife even more. So, what are some other events that you do with your family?

Family barbecue party 'Ask the Stars'

Mentor: I considered various events to do with my family, but as everyone lives outside due to their jobs, I decided to have a regular family barbecue party called 'Ask the Stars'. Here, 'stars' means that everyone in the family is precious like stars. 'Ask' means asking each other's well-being face-to-face. The important thing is that we hold this party as a potluck style. Everyone should bring one grilling food that can be grilled at the barbecue, which is a great way to increase participation and have fun. It's very important to make everything regular and programmatic like this.

Visitor : Ah, I see. It's really diverse and cool. I want to do that too. By the way, earlier you mentioned that the Comlive's target is 3+1. What is the 1 in this case?

Mentor: Here, the 1 in 3+1 means there is one more important thing to do to run Comlive well. That is to make good use of the community programs in your area.

Utilize local community programs

Visitor : You mean the local community programs?

Mentor: When we talk about 'community', we can refer to a society or a local community. To run Comlive, the important thing is to find community programs that suit you and keep challenging yourself. Never underestimate the local community programs. There are various types of programs available, from those conducted by government-funded foundations, lifelong learning centers or universities nearby, religious groups, and more. They are regularly held. Men tend to use them less than women. However, if you get rid of the prejudice that only older people attend them, you will find many great programs. Participating in these programs and creating a life that you can naturally enjoy with the people there is also crucial for social life after retirement.

Visitor : Are you talking about the interaction with participants in local community programs?

Mentor: That's right. Active participation in local community programs is strongly recommended as one of the most desirable ways to feel psychological connection and a sense of belonging to the local community.

Visitor : You emphasized the importance of community programs. Could you provide some examples of programs that you have personally utilized?

Mentor: If I could give just two examples, one of my favorite hobbies right now is playing the drums. When I was first learning the basics, I used a nearby community program to learn the basics and now practice on my own through self-study. If I hadn't gone there, I would still be dreaming about playing the drums. It was such a great decision, I think. Another example is a sewing reform program offered at a lifelong learning center operated by the city. I'm learning sewing skills there, and it seems to be a good match for me as a hobby.

Visitor : I can understand why you would want to learn the drums, but I'm very interested in how you came to think of learning sewing. Can you share the reasons behind it?

Find a hobby that suits your preference

Mentor: There are many people who have the prejudice that sewing is not suitable for men. However, I think that sewing is a hobby that is more suitable for men. I have several reasons for this.

visitor : You mentioned that you have several reasons. What are they?

Mentor: The biggest reason is that I wanted to break the stereotype that some things are meant for men to do and others for women. The second reason is, once I started sewing, I realized it requires a lot of creative thinking. Sewing is like creating a piece of art. It's so satisfying. When I concentrate on it, it's like drawing a picture, and sometimes it feels like playing an music instrument. Eventually, I came to think of it as a wonderful form of art. It's also very productive. As I'll mention later, it's good to focus on productive activities during retirement. Another reason is that I want to give our future grandchildren the handmade gifts that I made myself. Isn't that cool?

Visitor : So, have you made a lot of pieces now?

Mentor: Those who have watched my YouTube channel know that I personally alter and resize my clothes. I also make products that can be utilized using various unused materials. Sometimes, I also receive requests for repairs from my wife.

Visitor : It's a really admirable challenge. Thinking about the pieces that you'll give to your future grandchildren is amazing. You're doing great!

Mentor: Thank you for your compliments. If you ever get the chance, you should try sewing. It has a surprisingly attractive charm. Alright then, let's wrap up talking about Comlive for now and move on to the next topic.

Visitor : Great. So far, you have provided a detailed explanation on how to prepare for Sollive and Comlive. Could you please explain to me the third area that I need to prepare for?

4

A life of endless challenges
(Challive)

Mentor: The third area of retirement preparation is Challive. This means preparing for a life of endless challenges even after retirement. While all four areas of retirement preparation are important for a balanced life, Challive is the most important because it is the area most closely related to a retiree's future direction.

4 areas of retirement preparation

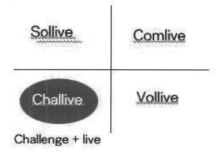

Visitor : Did you say that preparing for Challive is the area most closely related to a retiree's future direction?

Mentor: Yes, as I already explained, if we prepare well in the four areas of life for retirement, we can achieve almost perfect retirement preparation. However, I also mentioned that we may still feel that there is something missing. I referred to this as a 2% deficiency. Fulfilling this 2% deficiency and creating it as each person's core brand could be the goal of our future life. I explained that this means creating a self-core brand.

Visitor : Self-core brand? I'm not quite sure what that means. Can you explain it more specifically?"

Mentor: OK. By preparing well in the four areas of life for retirement, we can each discover the direction we most want to pursue. This becomes our self-core brand, which ultimately becomes the core direction or goal of our future life. It can even evolve into a second career after retirement. It's important to note that this is significantly different from short-term re-employment that may occur after retirement. Creating a self-core brand can bring great personal satisfaction and can be sustained over a long period of time, even becoming a lifelong career in some cases.

Create your own principles for Callive

Visitor : So, are you saying that you also prepared for Challive and were able to create your Self-core brand?

Mentor: That's right. So what I want to emphasize is that for retirees, how they prepare for Challive is very important. In other words, Challive can be the starting point for creating a new job in the later stages of life. Therefore, this field demands even more of our spirit of challenge. With a steady, consistent approach based on fundamental principles, I believe that each of us can achieve our own optimal and ideal goals in the desired direction.

Visitor : What principles do you follow in your work?

Mentor: I've come up with my own five principles. The first principle that I decided on is that learning a foreign language is the ultimate challenge that I cannot give up.

5 my principles for Challive

Learn New language	Aim for certificati- ons	Engage in SNS	Begin things promptly	Continuo- usly connect

Visitor : Did you say that learning a foreign language is your first principle?

Mentor: Because most people have studied various languages, including English, for a long time. In my case, I have also worked abroad in countries such as Canada for overseas branch assignment, and I have had the opportunity to study abroad for my MBA. However, so far, it seems that I have only studied languages for work-related purposes. Therefore, I decided to include learning a foreign language as my first principle because I thought it would be better to learn a language through voluntary learning after retirement, not for work purposes. And I also want to challenge myself with a new language that I haven't tried before, if possible.

Visitor : Seems like you are really drawn to the idea of learning a new language that you haven't tried before. I would like to give it a try as well. So, what is your second principle?

Mentor: My second principle is to aim for certification as a goal for the area of learning that I want to pursue, if possible. There are several benefits to this approach. First, it makes the goal clear. Second, in the preparation process for such certification, many parts require a knot at the beginning and the end, and one of the best ways to determine this is to obtain a certification. Obtaining a certification can be a motivating factor that is necessary in preparing for any activity.

Visitor : Until now, you have emphasized language and certification among the five principles. What is the third principle?

Mentor: The third principle is related to SNS. It is important not to neglect creating an infinite communication through SNS after retirement. The choice of which SNS to use may vary depending on personal preference, but I recommend that you pay a lot of attention to this aspect after retirement. Even if you were not interested in SNS before retirement, I recommend that you engage in various activities on SNS that suit you after retirement. Since the utilization methods and targets may vary depending on the type of each SNS, you need to constantly develop them to suit your own needs.

Visitor : You mentioned actively engaging in SNS activities that suit your personal interests and preferences after retirement. What about the fourth principle?

Mentor: The fourth principle of Challive is the importance of beginning in order to achieve the desires and goals that we want to pursue. This principle emphasizes the importance of starting. I consider this principle to be the most important motto in my life. When we have a dream that we want to achieve, it only becomes a reality when we take on the challenge. If we don't take on the challenge, it remains just a dream. A challenge only becomes a challenge when we begin. Therefore, starting is crucial.

Visitor : I completely agree with you. So, what is the final principle?

Mentor: The final principle is to continuously connect and pioneer the challenges we take on. As we overcome challenges, new ones that are constantly connected arise. It's never about achieving everything all at once from the beginning. Of course, there may be some trial and error, but through this process, we can create more new challenges and achieve even more.

Visitor : Ah, I see. So your point is that in order to live a life of continuously challenging oneself even after retirement, we need to establish five principles to follow.

Mentor: That's correct. However, these five principles are my own. I recommend that others create their own principles based on their own values and goals.

Visitor : You're saying that we should create our own principles. However, I just want to follow your principles. By the way, I'm curious about how you prepared for and carried out Challive.

Mentor: Sure. As for the first principle, I mentioned that learning a foreign language is the ultimate challenge that you shouldn't give up on, and I recommended trying to challenge yourself with a new language if possible. I think the idea of not giving up on learning a foreign language has several implications. The biggest one is that it acts as a powerful antidote to prevent self-esteem from easily collapsing after retirement by having the ability to study on your own. The second implication is that you can show your family, including your wife, grown-up children, and even your grandchildren, that you're always studying, which is a great example to set. Think about it. How wonderful is that?

Visitor : It's really cool to see someone studying even as they get older. However, there are many people who may want to learn a foreign language but feel like their minds are too rigid to do so. What do you suggest for those people?

Mentor: Don't put too much emphasis on any specific purpose or meaning for studying a foreign language after retirement. It's better to simply focus on the act of studying the language itself. It's not about going to a specific country to live or work, but simply enjoying the process of studying a foreign language day by day. If you start with the basics and study a little bit every day, you'll gradually build up your language skills without even realizing it.

Visitor : Now I understand. But why do you recommend learning a new language?

Mentor: Learning a new language requires starting from the basics, which is similar to starting a new life after retirement. Never be impatient and learn step by step from the basics. The most important thing is to keep going with persistence.

Visitor : So, what new language have you started studying?

Mentor: In that sense, after much consideration, I ultimately chose to learn Chinese. It's not easy to study Chinese, a language I knew nothing about, through self-study, but it's not entirely impossible either. There are so many good online programs that I believe you can enjoy learning a language through self-study. However, to increase the effectiveness and make your goals more tangible, I explained that it's advisable to aim for a certification. In my case, I set my goal to take the 'New HSK' Chinese proficiency exam, which is also a type of certification test. I passed levels 3 and 4, and I'm currently studying on levels 5 and 6. Once I complete the final stage, level 6, I plan to try learning a new language, Russian.

Visitor : Next is Russian! Wow! Impressive. So, what other Challive items are there?

Mentor: As for the second principle of Challive, I mentioned that it is good to aim for certification in the field you want to learn. Following this principle, I have obtained several certifications during my retirement preparation process. The first certification I challenged was the national certification for Western cooking, followed by the national certification for baking. When I was learning baking, I used to joke that my competitive rivals were high school students. In order to learn it at that time, I had to attend a private academy every day after work or use my vacation time, so there were some difficulties. However, I passed both the written and practical exams on my first try. In the baking field, I have set up a home bakery called "Kilimanjaro" in my space prepared for my retirement, where I bake bread myself. My favorite bread is a type of bread called "Stollen," which is mainly eaten during the Christmas season in Germany.

Visitor : You have a national certification as a baker and also operate a home bakery. That's impressive! What other certifications do you have?

Mentor: In addition, I have obtained certifications as a children's cooking instructor, POP and calligraphy instructor, and also a 1st-grade professional interviewer qualification. I sequentially obtained safety-related instructor certifications that I was interested in, such as Safety education instructor, Disaster safety instructor, Silver safety instructor, Children's safety instructor, and Psychological safety instructor. These certifications later became the background for me to work as a safety instructor. In connection with this, I obtained the qualification of a civil defense instructor and was selected as a civil defense education specialist instructor. Thus, I can say that the 12 certifications I obtained at the time became an important background for establishing my 'Self-core brand' after retirement.

Visitor : You obtained many certifications in a short period. Could you tell me more about the activities you engaged in related to the third principle?

Mentor: Yes, The third principle emphasizes the importance of communication through social media after retirement. However, most retirees are either disinterested or passive in this field. My suggestion is that retirees should actually strengthen their SNS activities after retirement. There are various types of SNS such as Facebook, Instagram, blogs, Naver Band, YouTube, etc. and the usage may vary depending on the type. What I want to emphasize is that retirees should have an active interest in utilizing these platforms more productively.

Visitor : You mentioned utilizing SNS more productively. Could you give me an example of how you have utilized it productively?

Blog is a shortcut to writing a book

Mentor: In my case, I've always wanted to start a blog after retirement. At that time, I thought that if I had something like a friend in my life after retirement, it would be music instrument. However, while thinking about what could be a companion that is closer to me than a friend, I thought that a blog might be the best way to express my thoughts. So, even though I had no knowledge about Blog, I started creating an account and setting it up by referring to other videos and resources. While considering what type of content to create for my Blog, I came up with a good idea.

Visitor : You mentioned having a good idea. What was it?

Mentor: Yes, I thought it would be great to provide guidance to retiree-to-be who may be struggling with how to prepare for retirement. So, I divided my Naver Blog categories into seven parts and started with the prologue "Retirement success lies in preparation," followed by an explanation of the four areas of retirement preparation and the concept of creating a 'Self-core brand'. I then added the contents of "My practical bucket list" and titled it "Preparing for Retirement," creating a wonderful and unique Blog.

Visitor : So, that became the background for the publication of your first book?

Mentor: That's correct. You are absolutely right. The content on this Blog became the basis for the birth of my first book. When I started this Blog, I had no intention of writing a book, but as I progressed with the Blog, I began to dream of turning it into a book.

Visitor : So, you went from blogging to publishing a book. That's impressive. So, do you engage in any other activities related to SNS, aside from your Blog?

Mentor: As my first example of SNS activity, I mentioned my challenge of writing a book using my Naver Blog. In addition to that, I engage in two other SNS activities. One is using Naver Band and the other is YouTube. I will explain my Naver Band activities in detail when I talk about the 'Vollive' part in the next section. For now, let me focus on YouTube.

Visitor : YouTube? That's interesting! I've been wanting to try it out, but I'm hesitant to start because I don't know where to begin. I'm really curious.

Mentor: First of all, I want to say that even retirees should boldly try to become a 'YouTube creator'. I want to emphasize that there are definitely many good things and reasons why retirees should operate a YouTube channel.

Visitor : It might not be easy for retirees to make up their minds to become a YouTuber. Why do you encourage such challenges?

Mentor: After retirement, I believe there are three reasons why retirees should become 'YouTube creators'. I call these three reasons the 'YouTube BTS'. You may have heard of BTS before. They are the name of the best K-pop group in Korea that recently topped the Billboard charts with hits like 'Dynamite' and 'Butter'. I will explain these reasons using the name BTS.

The reason to become a YouTuber : BTS

Visitor : You mentioned 'YouTube BTS'?

Mentor: Yes, YouTube BTS. The first reason why retirees should do YouTube, represented by the 'B' in BTS, is Busy. In other words, it can make retirees busy during their too free and loose time after retirement. This can also mean a very 'creative busyness'. Being creative is important. The second reason, represented by the 'T' in BTS, is Turning point. It can be the 'turning point' that changes retirees' lives. Becoming a YouTuber can be a great opportunity to create a new turning point in life. Lastly, the 'S' in BTS stands for Self-esteem. I think that the biggest challenge for retirees is the loss of self-esteem. Becoming a YouTuber can be a very effective means of preventing this potential loss of self-esteem and boosting confidence in retirement life.

YouTube BTS

Visitor : I see. I'm very curious about what motivated you to start YouTube and the type of content you've been creating so far. Can you please give me a brief introduction?

The gift that COVID-19 gave me

Mentor: To be honest, I've been thinking about starting a YouTube channel for a long time, and it's also been on my 'Bucket list' as item number 28. However, I never really had the courage to take on this challenge, and I thought it was something I wouldn't be able to do until I die. But unexpectedly, COVID-19 gave me a big gift. At that time, I mainly gave lectures to employees of companies or government officers who were preparing to retire, and I was quite satisfied with my progress. But suddenly, I encountered a setback, which was the COVID-19 pandemic. As a result, about 70 lectures that were scheduled for the first half of the year after my retirement were all canceled. It was a huge pain for me, just like it was for many other people. I couldn't express it easily, but it was really difficult. I sat alone in my office every day, waiting for COVID-19 to end, and it was driving me crazy. That's why I thought I couldn't waste this time and decided to take on the challenge I thought was the most impossible for me - becoming a one-person YouTube creator.

Visitor : It seems that COVID-19 became an opportunity for you to start on YouTube. I imagine it was difficult at first.

Mentor: Since I had to learn everything on my own, it felt very frustrating at first and I thought it would be a long way to go. However, I bought a few books about YouTube and learned step by step through other YouTube videos. After consistently learning the basics for about four months, I started to get the hang of it and realized that it wasn't as difficult as I thought. So, I created my YouTube channel called 'Eun-jun-in TV' with the title 'How This Man Enjoys Life After Retirement' in the channel art, and started making videos one by one. I also purchased the necessary equipment and as my skills improved, I thought about helping people who wanted to learn about YouTube even as they got older. That's why I created a video lecture series titled 'Anyone Can Become a YouTuber' divided into about 20 lectures and uploaded them as video lectures. In particular, I created the first-ever 'YouTube Map' that shows the entire process of YouTube and uploaded it with a separate explanatory video.

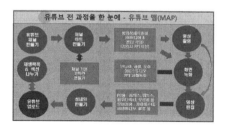

Visitor : YouTube Map? Could you tell me more about that?

Mentor: Yes, the YouTube Map. It's like a map that shows the entire process of creating a YouTube channel, from planning to shooting, editing, and uploading in one glance.

Visitor : I would love to see it too. Anyway, you not only learned about YouTube, but also created videos teaching others about YouTube.

Mentor: As a result, I received numerous requests for YouTube lectures from various places after uploading those lecture videos. In particular, YouTube lectures became another subject of my lectures, such as giving a special lecture to young employees working at the Gyeongju Art Hall titled 'Anyone Can Become a YouTube Creator'.

Visitor : I see. It seems that it is not so difficult and anyone can do it if they do it steadily. Then, I'm curious about the content of your YouTube channel. What kind of content does it mainly include?

Mentor: My YouTube channel includes various contents related to retirement. It contains various types of lectures, including author's lectures on my book 'Eun-Jun-in'. Many of my post-retirement activities are divided into 10 categories, with about 300 videos uploaded. It includes all the activities of the '4 Areas of Retirement Preparation' that I have explained so far. The content is very diverse, ranging from various types of lectures, songs I wrote, drum and shoulder keyboard instrument performance, cooking, baking, sewing, and other hobby activities.

Visitor : By the way, I'm curious about your YouTube performance. Could you tell me more about it?

60s YouTuber with 2M views video

Mentor: Since my YouTube channel includes such a diverse range
of content, I didn't initially gain many subscribers. But now,
I have over 13,000 subscribers and counting. It wasn't
easy to get to this point, but I've persevered. One of my
videos has gained a lot of popularity and has more than 2
million views.

Visitor : Wow! 2 million views? That's incredible! But I'm also
curious about your YouTube earnings.

Mentor: To be honest, when I first started YouTube, I was
desperate to achieve the milestone of 1,000 subscribers
and 4,000 watch hours, which I believe is every beginner
YouTuber's dream goal. This is because from this point
on, it is possible to generate income from YouTube. I
achieved this milestone in just 8 months, and I also had
some popular videos that generated a certain amount of
income. However, my purpose in doing YouTube is not to

make money, but rather to create a video diary of my retirement life, which is a bigger concept for me. So, I am just focusing on consistently making YouTube videos. Nevertheless, generating income from YouTube is always an area of interest for me. There are times when I earn a decent amount of money, but it is not always consistent. In fact, it is not easy for YouTubers to generate high income in general. For me, I am not too worried about the income and I am just focusing on leaving behind good quality videos that I have created. I strongly recommend anyone to try being a YouTuber. I believe that anyone can do it if they set their mind to it, even after retirement.

Visitor : After listening to your words, I also feel the courage to try YouTube. I will visit 'Eun-Jun-in TV' soon to explore the world of YouTube. So far, you have talked about the importance of communication through SNS as the third principle of Challive's five principles. Now, let's talk about the 4th principle. What is your story regarding the 4th principle?

Touch your dream to make it real

Mentor: Challive's fourth principle is 'Dreams only come true when they are pursued'. This may sound abstract, but I want to emphasize that this principle is both important and concrete. Everyone has dreams they want to achieve. However, these dreams remain just dreams if they are not pursued, and cannot become a reality. In other words, dreams can only be realized through challenge. The important thing is that these challenges can only happen when there is a start. Here, the concept of starting refers to a specific beginning. In other words, only through a specific beginning can the dream ultimately be realized.

Visitor: In a way, this is a very ordinary principle, but you emphasize it quite strongly.

Mentor: That's correct. Perhaps this is a very ordinary principle, but there is a reason why this ordinary principle is included in the five principles of Challive retirement preparation. We have constantly challenged ourselves towards our dreams and goals throughout our lives. Until now, we have taken various actions under various motivational factors. In other words, to put it simply, we have carried out everything under a lot of attention.

Visitor : That's true. But the situation will be quite different after retirement, won't it?

Mentor: That's right. After retirement, these situations will be completely different. External interference disappears and even attention fades away. In such a changed situation, it is not easy to challenge oneself towards a goal. Even if you try to set a goal and challenge yourself, it is difficult to get started. Ultimately, compared to the past, it is not easy to be motivated. Therefore, after retirement, it should be a very important principle that the beginning is crucial, and that the beginning must be specific.

Only a specific beginning is a start

Visitor : That's right. You mentioned that there should be a specific start after retirement. So, what specific start have you taken?

Visitor: I, too, have often felt that it's not easy to challenge oneself towards a goal during the retirement preparation process. Especially, I know that starting something can be really difficult. So, what I thought was to carefully set my goals, but attack them aggressively once they're set. That's why I made specific starting my fourth principle. Under this principle, I have accomplished some meaningful things myself. Anyway, as a retirement preparation specialist, I often introduce my experience and real-life examples. However, these are just examples, and I would like to emphasize again that retirees should find what suits them best.

Visitor : I completely agree with your advice to find what suits each individual. However, I think learning about your case could be very helpful for many people as well.

Mentor: Let me tell you. In fact, I will briefly mention writing a book as my first item related to the fourth principle. As I explained earlier, I didn't think about writing a book from the beginning when I retired. However, during the process of running my Naver Blog, I found that the Blog format was very suitable for writing a book. I also thought it would be great to share my research and experience on retirement preparation with many other people who are preparing for retirement. So, I decided to write a book. I changed the format of the Blog to the outline of a book and started writing. That was the concrete starting point for me to write a book. I copied the completed Blog by category and made it into a book format file, which I submitted to the publisher. At first, I had many concerns about whether I could make a book and how to create a lot of manuscript volume. However, because I had a concrete starting point, which was my Blog, I thought it was possible. The book that was born this way became the first practical guidebook for retirement preparation in Korea called 'Eun-jun-in'. I think it has become the most reliable support for me in my retirement life.

Visitor : That's really amazing. Can you give me another example?

Mentor: There was something else I really wanted to do. As I approached retirement, I wanted to give my wife and children a special gift to show my gratitude for all their support over the years. I wanted to create a unique song that would be the only one of its kind in the world as a gift. This became item 21 and 22 on my 'Practical Bucket List.' To write the lyrics for my wife's song, I purchased two books on lyric writing and began studying. For my son, I decided to create a rap and started to work on it. In order to make a rap, I needed to learn more about it, so I watched rap programs on TV such as 'Show Me The Money' and 'High School Rapper' to think about what kind of content to create. Ultimately, I decided to create a real-life story and wrote a rap that conveyed a message from a father to his son, inspired by a difficult situation that occurred when my twins were born in the hospital.

Visitor : So, did you succeed in creating the song and rap?

Mentor: Yes, it took about five months to complete. For my wife's song, I tried to capture the gratefulness I've felt towards her since we first met up until retirement in the lyrics. After much consideration, I decided to title it 'My Wife Inside Me.' I then had the lyrics composed and vocals recorded, and on our anniversary, October 30th, I gifted the completed song to my wife as the first single release. Now, it can be heard on various music platforms including YouTube.

내 안에 있는 내 아내

김 기 박

Visitor : 'My Wife Inside Me' is such a beautiful title. I would love to listen to it. Let's listen to the song right now.

Mentor: Let's do that. Let's have a cup of tea and listen to the song together.

The man turned on 'My Wife Inside Me' on YouTube from his PC. The gentle melody started with the lyrics, 'With your long hair swaying, you walked towards me and slightly tilted your head. In that moment, everything in the world felt mystical. Someone had penetrated into me'. The clear voice of a male singer conveyed the song. In that moment, the visitor thought that the person in front of him was truly living a warm life, experiencing and practicing life to its fullest. The visitor felt even more curious about the many stories that would unfold with this person in the future.

Visitor : The song is really good. I wonder how much your wife liked this song as a gift. I'm so curious about the next part. How did the rap for the twin sons go?

Mentor: The rap for my twin sons was really difficult to write, but after overcoming all obstacles, I finally completed the rap with the help of a professional rapper and even recorded a song as a final product. I gifted it to my twin sons and it became a significant turning point that brought us closer together. If I hadn't started writing this rap, I don't think it would have been possible to create a rap as a gift for my sons at the age of 60. I also made a video of this rap and uploaded it to my YouTube channel. Now, I'm practicing the rap with my sons to make an album and even create a music video together.

Visitor : Are you currently practicing with your twin sons to make this music album together? You truly are a challenger. Now I understand why you talk about a life of endless challenges. I saw a news article recently that you're also active as a lyricist. Is that true?

My lyricist debut, a life bonus

Mentor: That's right. Writing lyrics for my wife and children became an opportunity for me to debut as a lyricist during the free time of COVID-19 pandemic. It was an unexpected bonus in my life. As a result, the songs I wrote have been produced as digital singles and are being sold on music streaming services. Following my first song, 'My Wife Within Me,' 'The Tom Sky,' 'Gyeongju Arirang,' 'Than Audrey Hepburn,' and 'The Brown Mask' have been released as an album. In addition, there are more than ten lyrics waiting to be released. I also made video music for each song at no cost and registered them on music streaming services. I learned and carried out various planning tasks for music release on my own.

Visitor : Ah, I see. But I recently heard that one of the songs you've written the lyrics has been rising as a representative song of Gyeongju City. Is that true?

Mentor: Although it may not be considered as the official representative song of Gyeongju yet, it is clear that "Gyeongju Arirang" has risen to become a representative song of the city. Every June 8th is designated as Gyeongju Citizen's Day, and a large festival is held to celebrate. This song is sung on the main stage of the festival, indicating that it is becoming a representative song of Gyeongju. Many people love 'Gyeongju Arirang' because they felt that there was no song that truly represented Gyeongju after 'Moonlit Night in Shilla Dynasty.' Now, I am very happy and grateful that this song is being performed on many big stages, including the Gyeongju Art Center, and at various events.

Visitor : You are truly amazing. I also hope that the day when 'Gyeongju Arirang' represents Gyeongju comes soon. I also heard that you recently received a big award related to your lyrics.

Mentor: Yes, my work 'Yegiso' won the grand prize at a recent nationwide lyric competition. I felt really good to be recognized as a lyricist.

Visitor : You received a really big award at the nationwide lyric competition. Congratulations! You have truly become a professional lyricist. You really have boundless talent, don't you? It doesn't seem like something anyone can do. It's something that I couldn't even dream of doing myself.

Mentor: Many people say that. I also know that each of these things is not easy to achieve. But even though I only talk about the results, the process was not easy at all. But the important thing is that just a few years ago, I had nothing. I didn't even know what I was good at, what I wanted, or even what I liked. I think anyone can do it if they do a little bit of what they want every day.

Visitor : Ah, I see. I'll remember that. Could you explain the fifth principle then?

Mentor: The fifth principle is 'consistently explore the area you want to challenge.' Although all of Challive's principles are important, this fifth principle is closely related to the future direction of retirees. Especially after we talk about the '4 areas of retirement preparation', the topic of developing a 'Self-core brand' will be closely related.

Visitor : It would be great if you could explain more about that.

Mentor: Even if someone has a field they want to challenge, it is unlikely that any field will be accomplished in one shot or in a short period of time. Therefore, it is important to consistently find the links towards that target. To explain more simply, when we face the specific implementation stage for the selected activities in the '4 areas of retirement preparation,' if a more interesting and specific field is discovered during the process, we need to differentiate that field and eventually commercialize, specialize, and even professionalize it. This is ultimately about creating a Self-core brand for retirement and even connecting it to a career. I want to emphasize that this is something anyone can do with just a little interest and challenge.

Visitor : You mentioned that in the retirement preparation process, we should utilize the links well for the specific fields of interest discovered and move towards commercialization, specialization, and professionalization. Could you give me a specific example of yourself?

Mentor: You came all the way here to hear about it, so I should certainly let you know. Let me briefly tell you about my representative case of developing a specific field discovered into specialization and professionalization. As an example, I will take becoming a lecturer. I went through various considerations in the retirement preparation process, but I was particularly interested in becoming a lecturer. The problem was what content to teach. I thought I should challenge a field that others cannot easily access. Finally, I decided to specialize in the retirement field based on the book I wrote. I continued to study in that field by not only reading other people's books and papers but also attending online and offline lectures on related topics. In addition, I prepared for lectures, such as creating a PPT based on my book's content. Also, in order to specialize in this field, I received the title of 'Retirement preparation practical expert' from a related coaching association, and after considering what to call it, I decided to name it 'ART Coach,' which includes the abbreviation ART, meaning after retirement. I became the 'first ART Coach' in Korea. Through this preparation process, I started my main activities as a lecturer.

Visitor : I can feel the process of becoming more specialized. You emphasized the importance of connections. Have you also looked for connections in other areas related to your lectures?

Mentor: Of course. My lecture activities led to teaching courses for retirees at local governments, universities, and lifelong learning centers. In addition, I collaborated with retirement education institutions to participate in retirement programs for corporate retirees, such as Hello! My life. And I submitted an essay titled "The Gift of COVID-19 to My Life" to a certain competition and unexpectedly won a big prize. As a result, I appeared on the MBC radio campaign program "Starting the Second Half of Life" to encourage retirees nationwide. Another unforgettable moment was my live appearance on the TBN Transportation Broadcast for almost a year during the morning commute, sharing my story about retirement preparation. I consider this opportunity to be more valuable than anything else.

Visitor : It's really dynamic. I think I can understand the concept of connecting ideas very well. Writing a book, giving lectures based on that book, connecting to other lectures, and even broadcasting - it's such a wonderful connection. And it's amazing that you made several songs, including the song for your wife and the representative song for Gyeongju, and even produced and released an album for the songs. That's really impressive! By the way, how is the income from selling the music?

Mentor: It's difficult to expect a large income since I haven't started that long. But still, it's amazing that money comes into my account from selling music. It's something that I couldn't even imagine a few years ago, right? I don't think I'm particularly talented in this area. I just believe that anyone can do it if they challenge themselves and use the concept of connecting ideas, little by little. I want to clearly say that it's something that anyone can do.

Visitor : Anyway, you're amazing. Maybe you're even busier after retirement. However, I'm curious if there were any cases where you failed during Challive. Have there been any?

A valuable victory despite the failure

Mentor: Of course. When I share my own challenge stories, many people may think that I succeeded in everything, but in fact, there were many difficulties during the process, and there were also several cases of failure. Let me share one of those cases. I used to be unhappy with the fact that only young people's emoticons were available on KakaoTalk whenever I used my phone. I wondered why there were no suitable emoticons for older people. As a result, I decided to challenge myself to create my own emoticons and try to sell them. It was not an easy task. It took about six months to reach the final stage of proposing my emoticons to Kakao Emoticon Studio, including learning Photoshop, which was essential for the project. However, I failed because of illegal font usage. I thought I could use any free font on my PC, but later I found out that there were some fonts that could not be used for commercial purposes. Although this challenge failed, I consider it the most valuable victory I gained at the age of 60 in all my challenges. I could feel great joy even through this failure.

Visitor : Your words about achieving a valuable victory despite your failure really touched me. So, to summarize, could you tell me about Calllive and then we can move on to the next topic?

Mentor: In my opinion, Challive, which keeps challenging endlessly, seems to be independent of retirement or age. My conclusion is that if I hesitate to start something when I'm at the starting point, I won't be able to do what I really want to do. Therefore, while having a goal and a dream is important, and while cultivating a challenging spirit to achieve that dream is also important, I think it's ultimately important to boldly take the starting point when you decide to take on the challenge. In the end, I want to say that the concrete starting point of how you take that beginning is the most important. Do you see the phrase on my desk? 'Thinking is not doing.' That's my favorite life motto, meaning that nothing can be accomplished just by thinking.

visitor : That's a really nice sentence. You explained Challive so well. Now, only the final area of Vollive remains, and I am very curious. Alright! Then please tell me about Vollive, the final area.

5

A life enjoying volunteering
(Vollive)

Mentor: So far, we have talked about Sollive, Comlive, and Challive, the first three areas of retirement preparation. Now, let's talk about the final stage, 'Vollive'. In short, Vollive is about preparing for a life of enjoying volunteering. Vollive plays a very important role in retirement life and is essential. During my research on retirement preparation, I conducted a survey on the most desirable way of life after retirement. As a result, over 80% of the respondents answered that the most desirable way of life after retirement is a happy life. I could empathize with that result. So, I investigated what specific conditions need to be met to lead a happy life, and I thought that there might be about five main factors, which I call the 'Five F's of Happiness'.

4 areas of retirement preparation

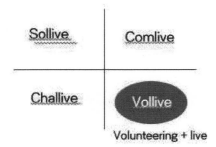

Volunteering + live

5F+α that create happiness

Visitor : What are the five elements of the Five F's of Happiness?

Mentor: Among the five elements starting with F, the first F is Finance, which means money. Simply put, to be happy, you need money. The second F is Fitness, which means health. This is something that everyone can relate to. The third F is Field, which refers to work or hobbies. What do you think the fourth F is? It's Friends, which means the personal network of friends. Finally, the last F is Fun, which means happiness through fun or interest. In other words, life must be more interesting and enjoyable to be happy.

5 F's of Happiness

Finance

Fitness

Field

Happiness
(5F's)

Friends

Fun

Visitor : You summarized the five elements of happiness into 5F: Finance, Fitness, Field, Friends, and Fun. These represent money, health, work, friends, and enjoyment, respectively.

Mentor: That's right. All five of these elements are important. That's why I've made it my life goal to live a happy life after retirement. However, upon careful consideration, I realized that the concept of happiness is mostly based on comparison. In other words, people's satisfaction with happiness is greatly influenced by comparing themselves to others. They believe they need to live in a better apartment than others, own a better car or more expensive luxury goods to feel happy, their spouse needs to have a better job or a higher position to feel happier, and their children need to attend a better university to feel happier. I felt that this emphasis on happiness through comparison, rather than the small and simple joys in life, was not ideal. This made me think about what an ideal life after retirement should look like, instead of just pursuing happiness.

What does your ideal life look like?

Visitor : So did you find what your ideal life after retirement looks like?

Mentor: Yes, I found it. At first, it was difficult to find. I wondered what life would be like if it weren't a happy life. I thought about a healthy life, a meaningful life, a joyful life, a considerate life, and a challenging life, and the last word I came up with was dignity. The word 'dignity' resonated with me because it embodies both grace and formality. This led me to the conviction that a life with dignity is the most ideal way to live after retirement. So, what should I do to live a life with dignity? It doesn't have to be something revolutionary, but there should be something. In other words, the 5F conditions of happiness are good, but is there something else that can be added to them? While pondering this, I thought of volunteering. In other words, volunteering should always be of interest, but especially after retirement, one should live a life of enjoying volunteering.

Visitor : I see. However, I believe that there are some principles to follow while living a life of enjoying volunteering. Is there such a thing as principles?

Mentor: I wrote in detail about it in my first book 'Eun-Jun-in', but there are also three principles in Vollive. Let me explain each of the three principles in detail.

Visitor: You mentioned that you have three principles for volunteering. Could you please explain those principles in detail?

Volunteering starts from home

Mentor: Okay. It seems that it would be good to follow only these three principles. The first principle of Vollive is that volunteering begins at home. While working in the field of volunteering for a long time, I realized that many people perceive volunteering as something that can only be done outside. Of course, it is important to come out into society and engage in volunteer activities. However, I would like to emphasize that volunteering should start from home, especially after retirement.

3 principles of vollive

Start from home	Diverse Community service	Regular community volunteering

Visitor : I see. However, why is it especially important to volunteer at home after retirement?

Mentor: There are good reasons for that. After retirement, couples need to place more emphasis on their relationship. Recently, the trend of divorce after the age of 50 has been increasing by more than 10% every year. The reason for this is that a husband's retirement has a big impact on his wife. In other words, when a husband retires and becomes a 'three meals a day' husband, the risk of depression for the wife with such a husband is 70% higher than before, according to data. That's why the illness that occurs in wives with retired husbands is called 'Retired Husband Syndrome'.

Visitor : So there's such a thing as 'Retired Husband Syndrome'?

Mentor: Yes, there is such a thing as Retired Husband Syndrome. To explain it in a different way, traditionally, the home is considered a woman's space. However, even if the husband's retirement is expected, the return of the husband to the home can be perceived as an unwelcome intruder who invades the wife's space without notice. From the wife's perspective, if the husband ignores the many rules she has established in the living space and insists on sharing the space after retirement, it would be very difficult for the wife to accept. It can be a big source of stress for the wife and can gradually worsen into a bigger illness. Thinking that my wife will not feel this way is a great misconception on the part of the husband.

Visitor : I see. As a husband, it may be hard to accept, but it is a valid point. So what mindset should a retired husband adopt?

Mentor: I asked a man who is turning 60, and he said he had

asked to write down what he wants to do most after retirement on his bucket list. Almost all of them wrote that they want to travel overseas with their wife, who has gone through a lot with them, as the first thing. Before retirement, I also participated in a retirement preparation program called 'Bravo! My Life' and was asked to write down three things I want to do on my bucket list. I wrote that down as the first thing, too. However, the important thing is that when we ask wives, they want to travel overseas with their friends or children, not just with their husbands. It may be a sad story from a husband's perspective, but we must admit that the world has already changed like this. Therefore, even if a couple lives within one fence, they should see each other as one independent individual. It seems very clear that the relationship between a couple heading for old age can be smooth only when each individual recognizes each other's world.

Visitor: I see. What is the relevance of that to the saying 'volunteering starts at home'?

Mentor: After retirement, when the husband returns home, it means that he needs to make efforts as a same kind of family member. It is crucial to not disrupt the framework of the home that wife have maintained all along. The attempt to make the home revolve around himself as the center after the husband's retirement is deemed highly risky. Therefore, the retired husband should show himself as a participant in the new image of the family, and expressing it in the form of volunteering for the home is a very natural way to do so. Especially, the husband's service to his wife cannot be anything but a meaningful commitment to the family, starting a new phase of life after retirement.

Visitor : What do you think is the best way to serve the family at home?

Mentor: Volunteering for the family is also important to set specific goals. It is recommended to specify the items for volunteering and declare them specifically through 'Declare'. Instead of making vague declarations like 'I will volunteer well,' it is better to declare and proceed with specific actions for the benefit of the home, my family, and my spouse.

Visitor : Your point about making specific declarations for volunteer work is very impressive. So, what was the first item you declared for Vollive?

Mentor: I chose my wife as the first beneficiary of my 'Vollive' journey. While I was working, I often neglected my wife, using my job as an excuse. However, even after retirement, I wanted to volunteer and do something for my wife, even if it was just a little. That's why I decided to develop an item specifically for my wife. At first, I wasn't sure what kind of volunteering I should do, and I pondered over it for a long time. But then, every time I cooked a meal for her and saw how happy it made her, I realized that this was it. So, I included 'Cooking for my wife' as the first item on 'my practical bucket list'.

1st item on my practical bucket list?

Visitor : Is the first item on your bucket list?

Mentor: However, I don't just call it a 'bucket list,' I refer to it as a 'practical bucket list.' A practical bucket list is a bucket list that includes a strong will to actually carry out the items on the list. For my practical bucket list, I decided that the first item would be to 'cook 500 dishes for my wife until I die.' I did have some concerns about 500 dishes too many, but since we are now living in the age of 100, I thought I would give it my best shot and take on the challenge.

Visitor : Wow! 500 dishes until you die? That's impressive! So, how did you go about it specifically?

Mentor: I first obtained certifications in Western cuisine and baking to specifically cater to my wife's favorite dishes and bread. I started cooking for my wife and family in earnest. As the first dish, I began making hamburger. I still vividly remember the moment when my wife and children said it was delicious and suggested opening a burger restaurant.

Visitor : It looks like your family really enjoyed it. So, how many dishes have you made up until now?

Mentor: I have made over 300 dishes so far, but I still have a long way to go to reach 500.

Visitor : Making 500 dishes is truly impressive. I, on the other hand, only know how to boil ramen. But I imagine that as you continue this journey, you must have many memorable moments. If there is one that stands out, what would it be?

Mentor: The most memorable moment for me was when I turned 60 and decided to host a birthday party by preparing the food myself and inviting my family. On that day, I prepared garlic steak as the main dish. I also baked apple pies, enough for everyone in the family, and it seemed like everyone was deeply touched. My wife mentioned that it was the first time in the world for someone to personally cook and bake for his own 60th birthday celebration, and she was deeply moved by it. It was truly a meaningful occasion for me as well.

Visitor : You personally cooked and baked bread for your 60th birthday celebration and invited your family That's truly impressive. Anyway, I hope the 500 dishes turn out well. Now, let's move on to the second principle.

Volunteering with various talents

Menor: The second principle is that there are diverse ways to serve the community. Therefore, let's each find unique volunteer activities that suit us. The essence of this statement is that we often tend to think of volunteering solely as physical activities, but volunteering is not limited to physical service alone. The methods of volunteering can be incredibly diverse. Especially after retirement, it can be very meaningful to find various forms of volunteer activities that utilize one's abilities, experiences, and skills to the fullest. For example, if someone retired as a police officer, they could engage in volunteer activities related to child traffic safety. It is important to find creative volunteer opportunities that align with one's interests, abilities, hobbies, talents, and experiences.

Visitor : Your advice is to find volunteer activities that are related to our abilities or experiences. Do you have any volunteer activities that you engage in as well?

Mentor: First, I would like to mention that anyone can engage in meaningful volunteer activities by using the most of their hobbies, abilities, and experiences. With that in mind, let me cautiously share my own example. I have a few volunteer ideas that align with my interests and abilities. While discussing the second principle of the Challive's five principles, which is to utilize SNS for communication after retirement, I mentioned that I would provide more detailed information about Naver Band later on Vollive. Now, I will explain the content to you.

Visitor : How will Naver Band and Vollive be connected?

Operating the Best Foodie Naver Band

Mentor: I manage various tasks through Naver Band, and among them, there is one large-scale band that I have been running for nearly 10 years. It started as a small family band with four members, but now it has become arguably the best large-scale foodie band in a single region in Korea. This band is called 'Gyeong-o-muk', which means "What to eat in Gyeongju?" in the local dialect. People who run restaurants in Gyeongju are likely to know about it, and I believe that most interested citizens are also aware of it. However, apart from a few close acquaintances who are my family and close friends, very few people know that I am the operator of this band.

Visitor : It is said that the phrase 'What should we eat in Gyeongju today?' is shortened to 'Gyeong-o-muk.' They are referred to as the best large-scale band in a single region. How many people are currently members, and how is it being operated?

Mentor: This band currently has morn than 20,000 members. Initially, it was mostly centered around the residents of Gyeongju, but recently, there has been a significant increase in the number of tourists joining. This band specifically targets restaurants in Gyeongju, and both customers and restaurant owners can leave reviews or promotional posts. The information shared is accessible to all members of the band. When someone posts a message, it quickly reaches around 1,000 people, creating a tremendous promotional effect. It can be described as a large-scale band with powerful advertising impact.

Visitor : Morn than 20,000 people? That's a significant promotional effect. I'm curious how you have managed to keep running this band.

Mentor: As I mentioned before, initially it was just me and my family, four of us, sharing restaurant photos and memories on our family band. People around us found it interesting and kept asking to join, so one by one, more members started joining, and it expanded to this scale. The primary purpose of me running this band was to share healthy dining culture information with all members. Furthermore, it was a way to provide some assistance to small restaurant owners who are struggling in difficult local economic conditions. Moreover, I believe that through this Gyeong-o-muk band, I can contribute to the revitalization of tourism in Gyeongju, a tourist city. Nowadays, among young tourists, it is said that when they come to Gyeongju, they don't have to worry about where to eat as long as they check Gyeong-o-muk. For these activities, I have to dedicate a considerable amount of time each day to manage the band, but I consider it as an important volunteer work without a face.

Visitor : It's a really great volunteer activity that also contributes to the tourism industry in Gyeongju. I should join the band and use it with my family when we visit Gyeongju next time. So, what is the last third principle?

Mentor: The third principle of Vollive is to participate in community volunteering on a regular basis after retirement. It emphasizes that it can be challenging to commit to such regular community volunteering activities unless you make a conscious effort to do so. You may wonder how significant community volunteering after retirement can be, but it plays a crucial role in ensuring a more dignified and healthy post-retirement life. Engaging in regular volunteering activities is essential for a more fulfilling and meaningful life after retirement.

Visitor : So, to ensure a more dignified post-retirement life, it is essential to participate in community volunteering activities regularly. What kind of community volunteering activities do you think would be good after retirement?

Mentor: Well, there isn't a one-size-fits-all answer to that. As I mentioned before, it's best to consider your own career, skills, or preferred hobbies when choosing community volunteering activities. In reality, there are plenty of options available in your surroundings. For example, you could consider physical volunteering at a nearby facility for people with disabilities, a nursing home, a children's center, or a soup kitchen. Alternatively, you could offer your talents in performing arts, such as playing music or doing magic tricks. You could also volunteer at various local events. It's all about considering your preferences and available time. If you're having trouble deciding, you can always reach out to the local volunteer center in your area. They should be able to provide you with ample guidance. Additionally, it's often a good idea to join a volunteer organization that aligns with your interests, as participating alongside other members can provide a sustainable way to continue your volunteering efforts.

Visitor : There are so many different activities that are possible. However, why is it important to participate in these volunteer activities after retirement?

Main purpose of volunteering after retirement

Mentor: That's a great question. Actually, I have been thinking a lot about whether I really need to do this kind of volunteer work as I get older and retire. However, through my experiences, I have come to strongly feel that this kind of volunteer work is absolutely necessary for retirees. I think there are two main purposes to it.

Visitor : Did you say there are two main purposes to volunteering after retirement?

Mentor: Yes. The first purpose is for the enhancement of our lives after retirement. As I mentioned earlier, I decided to pursue a dignified life as my ideal life after retirement. To achieve a dignified life, I realized that volunteering for others is essential. It is necessary to start from home and expand to the local community by participating regularly. Then, your life will become much more heartwarming. Wouldn't that be a dignified life?

2 purposes of volunteering after retirement

Life enhancement	Self-discovery

Visitor : O.K. Volunteering for a dignified life is truly admirable. So, what is the second reason for participating in volunteer activities after retirement?

Mentor: The second reason is for self-discovery, which is found through personal experiences gained from volunteering. Actually, after retiring and turning 60, I thought I had become quite old. Of course, I didn't feel physically or mentally old, but I felt like I had aged quite a bit. However, after participating in social volunteer activities, those thoughts disappeared completely. Through these volunteer activities, I realized how young I still am. More importantly, I realized that there are still many things I need to do.

Visitor : Through volunteer activities, you felt like you could forget about your age and realized there are still many things to do. I'm curious about what kind of volunteer activities you are currently engaged in.

Mentor: I can't help but share my own case. There is always a cautious aspect when I talk about my case. However, I will share it for the purpose of this lecture. After retirement, I went out to the local community to find regular volunteer work that I could do myself, and I chose a free soup kitchen called 'Neighbor's House' where I had previous experience while I was working. I promised myself that I would come out regularly to volunteer after retirement. I registered the day after my retirement ceremony and started volunteering immediately because I wanted to keep that promise.

Visitor: It's impressive that you registered the day after your retirement ceremony to keep your promise. What kind of activities do you do at the free soup kitchen, and how is the current situation at the place?

Mentor: The place where I volunteer is a free soup kitchen that provides lunch to the less fortunate neighbors. Around two hundred people visit the place every day. About twenty volunteers come out daily to help with the service. The schedule involves preparing the food for lunch, doing dishes and cleaning up, and then returning in the afternoon. I have chosen Fridays as my regular day to go there. My main duty there is dishwashing.

Visitor : So you mean you'll be the main dishwasher? It seems like there will be a lot of dishes to wash in a bulk, right?

Mentor: Yes, my role there is the main dishwasher. Usually, three people work as a team for dishwashing, and the main dishwashing is the most critical position. It involves washing the dishes first with hot water. It's okay during the winter, but during the summer, I sweat like it's raining. After finishing work, my whole body is always drenched in sweat. It's a demanding job that requires tremendous strength and speed to handle a large amount of dishwashing in a short time, but I've been in charge of this position since the beginning. When I finish, I feel extremely happy. At first, it was a bit awkward, but as I kept doing it steadily every week, it became a part of my life, and I looked forward to the day of volunteering. There was a situation where it was suspended entirely due to COVID-19, and I was worried about whether the people who used to come would skip meals. I'm really grateful that it has resumed, and everything is back to normal.

Visitor : It seems like COVID-19 has also prohibited volunteering activities. I'm glad it has resumed, though. Do you feel a great sense of fulfillment?

Mentor: Yes, even though I am retired and living my second life, when I see the elderly at the volunteering site, I realize how young I still am and how much more I have to do. Being able to participate in volunteer activities like this brings immense happiness, and it also teaches me the value of life.

visitor : Indeed, your post-retirement life is filled with diverse and meaningful activities. I've heard some great solutions for retirement preparation so far. So, let's summarize the four areas of retirement preparation for a comprehensive understanding.

Mentor: Yes, I have emphasized that in order to have a successful retirement life, one needs to be well-prepared for retirement. This preparation involves finding activities in each of the four areas and balancing them. The first area is preparing for a fulfilling life enjoyed alone, called 'Sollive'.

The second is preparing for a life enjoyed together, called 'Comlive'. The third is preparing for a life of endless challenges, called 'Challive'. Lastly, it is about preparing for a life enjoyed through volunteering, called 'Vollive'. I have explained these principles with my own examples to help understand each aspect of life. Many people now understand that this kind of life preparation is not only applicable to retirees but can be followed by anyone.

Visitor : Yes, indeed. Regardless of whether you're a retiree or not, anyone who follows this approach can experience a significant improvement in his or her quality of life.

Mentor: Yes, indeed. This principle is not something that only retirees should follow. It can become a practical guideline that anyone can follow to change their quality of life. Now, let me explain how to build your self-core brand, which will be the core of your future, on this prepared framework.

Visitor : You mentioned that you will now talk about the self-core brand. I'm truly excited to hear your explanation.

Mentor: Are you curious? This is the essence of my lecture.

6

Create 'Self-core brand'

Mentor: Now, let's talk about Self-core brand. This will be the most essential part of my first book, Eun-Jun-in. Therefore, first, it is necessary to understand the concept of Self-core brand well, including what it is.

Visitor : Yes, that's right. So, how can we define Self-core brand?

Mentor: Self-core brand can be defined as creating a unique brand that aligns with one's own pursuit of the most essential work one want to engage in, in preparation for retirement. However, an important concept here is not just finding the core work but creating it anew. Thus, the concept of 'creation' which means producing something new is very important.

Visitor : It sounds a bit difficult for me. Could you please explain it in simpler terms?

Mentor: Let me explain it in simpler terms. It means that after retirement, in order to embrace the golden years of our lives, we need to find work that suits us and transform it into our core occupation. In other words, it can be divided into two stages. The first stage involves finding work that is suitable for ourselves. The second stage is about transforming that work into our core occupation. However, most of us retire without going through these processes while preparing for retirement. As a result, retirees often find themselves lost and wandering during their retirement years. If we go through these two stages, anyone can easily discover their core personal brand and live their golden years with more elegance and fulfillment.

Visitor : It is said that two stages are needed to create one's Self-core brand.

Go through the preparation process

Mentor: That's right. Imagine for a moment comparing someone who has gone through such a process to prepare for retirement with someone who has not. There will probably be a big difference. However, I think we are living under a great misconception. I don't believe that someone who has gone through such a process to prepare is necessarily an exceptional or extraordinary person. Perhaps that should be very natural. On the contrary, I would like to say that those who wander aimlessly after retirement without direction, without going through such a process, are not desirable. Therefore, it is essential for retirees to make efforts to have basic retirement preparation for our retirement life.

Visitor : Briefly, retirees need to go through a preparation process of finding and creating their own work to prepare for retirement. So why do we need to have a self-core brand?

Mentor: Many of us are worried about the uncertainties surrounding our future retirement. When we analyze the root causes, three main factors emerge : finances, health, and loneliness. This is something that resonates with a lot of people. So, what is the best way to address these concerns? The answer lies in finding meaningful 'work.' However, after spending a significant portion of our lives dedicated to a particular job, it may not be feasible to simply cling to any random activity after retirement. Instead, we need to search for work that fulfills us, at least to some extent. This process involves identifying suitable options and transforming them into our core pursuits. Ultimately, this can become a new vocation during our golden years or simply a cherished endeavor that aligns with our aspirations, even if it is not an occupation.

3 worries about the retirement years

Finances   Health   Loneliness

Visitor: Why do retirees tend to neglect retirement preparation, especially the creation of a self-core brand?

Why I wrote a retirement guidebook?

Mentor: This is a very important question. In my opinion, it's because the conditions for retirement preparation weren't there until now, and we didn't know how to prepare. That is, we were not given enough time to prepare for retirement due to the social structure. If we look at our immediate seniors, they worked until the day before retirement, attended a farewell party, and then the next day, they had to attend their retirement ceremony and go home. There was no time to prepare and even if they wanted to, they didn't know how to prepare. Because there was no practical guidebook that provided guidelines on what and how to prepare. That's why I wrote a practical guidebook on retirement preparation called 'Eun-jun-in', which means 'Retirement Planner'.

Visitor : Indeed, I understand. I felt the same way. So, even if someone wanted to prepare for retirement, there was a lack of practical guidelines, as you mentioned. So, how did retirees prepare for retirement in the past?

Mentor: Except for a few exceptional individuals, most people suddenly became unemployed overnight. They went from being employed to jobless in an instant. So, how did they avoid that situation? The easiest way was to prefer reemployment. According to recent statistics, 81.4% of retirees prefer reemployment as their primary job-seeking method. Entrepreneurship accounts for 16.6%, and unpaid volunteer work is at 2%. This shows that retirees naturally prefer reemployment. Moreover, it can be said that those with specialized skills have the highest probability of reemployment in the same industry.

Visitor : I see. As they are of a working age, it is natural for them to prefer reemployment, and especially in occupations where they have specialized expertise, wouldn't it be ideal for them to reenter that field?

Mentor: I'm not saying that reemployment is a bad thing. Those who are capable of reemployment should do so naturally. However, what's important is that there aren't many opportunities for reemployment, so it's very difficult for most people to find a new job. Especially for people like me who worked in office jobs, it's almost impossible. And even if you do manage to reenter the workforce, the period of employment is usually limited to around 2-3 years. But through my research, I discovered that there is a more important reason for reemployment than financial reasons.

Visitor : There are more important reasons for reemployment than economic ones, you say?

Mentor: That's right. Of course, even after retirement, everyone would want to work again to make more money. However, the more important reason behind it is the lack of proper retirement preparation. Without adequate preparation for retirement, people often become increasingly anxious as retirement approaches because they don't know what to do or how to spend their time. Especially as the head of the family, there is a fear of losing one's status and position that they have worked hard to maintain for their family. However, everyone still wants to be recognized and appreciated by their family. They want to send a message to their family that even after 30 years of working hard for them, they are still working hard through reemployment. That's why they hope to work even harder. Of course, there is no bad intention behind it. However, since that period is not very long, even if reemployment extends their active service period, they will eventually have to retire and face retirement. In the end, retirement preparation is necessary at some point, and it's better to start preparing for it as early as possible.

Visitor : So, how should 'Self-core brand', as you emphasized, be created?

Mentor: It's a really important question. To put it simply, what we need to understand is that finding 'Self-core brand' is not something that happens overnight. It doesn't just suddenly fall from the sky one day. It can be born through a process of preparing for a balanced life, and that process involves being well-prepared in the '4 areas of retirement preparation'. It is through this journey that a self-core brand can be created.

Creation of Self-core brand

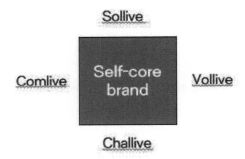

Visitor : I see. So, there is a deep relationship between the 'Self-core brand' and the '4 areas of retirement preparation'.

Mentor: That's right. Through preparation for Sollive, Comlive, Challive, and Vollive, within a framework of a balanced life, one can discover the direction they should pursue and create it as their own, forming a self-core brand. This can even expand into a second career. Ultimately, it is about finding something that one enjoys and is good at, and sustaining it for a long time.

Visitor : Okay. I understand it well enough. Now, I think we need a more detailed explanation on how to create such 'Self-core brand'. Is there any specific procedure or method for that?

How to build a Self-core brand

Mentor: Of course, there is. I am explaining the process of building 'Self-core brand' in 5 steps. The first step is the detailed planning phase for the '4 areas of retirement preparation'. The second step is the execution phase for each area. The third step is the focus phase, where you concentrate on the areas of interest. The fourth step is the phase of devising a differentiation strategy for the chosen area. And finally, the fifth step is the phase of commercializing and specializing the 'Self-core brand'. Now, let me explain each step in detail.

5 steps of Self-core brand

Plan Phase of 4RP	Execution Phase of 4RP	Focus Phase of 4RP	Differentiation Phase of 4RP	Specialization Phase of SCB

(4RP : 4 areas of retire preparation / SCB : Self-core brand)

Visitor : You mentioned that the first step is the detailed planning phase for the '4 areas of retirement preparation'. Can you explain it in more detail?

Mentor: Yes, the first step is the detailed planning phase for the 4 areas of retirement preparation. Simply put, it is the initial phase of finding the items for the 4 areas that one wants to pursue after retirement. What do you want to do after retirement, and what do you need to do? How much of each area should be included in the plan? How can you realize the activities as items for each area? How long should the execution period be? It is a phase of devising specific plans for each activity in each area.

Visitor : I understand the concept of the execution method, but I'm still having trouble grasping how to specifically get started.

Mentor: Of course, it's understandable because you may have never approached retirement preparation in this way before. Through my coaching experience, I have encountered many people in this situation. Therefore, I am trying to convey the concrete methods that I have actually used as much as possible. Let me also tell you about the tool I used for this phase. First, to find activities for the 4 areas, draw a cross on a large piece of paper and divide it into four sections. Then, write 'Sollive' on the top left, 'Comlive' on the top right, 'Challive' on the bottom left, and 'Vollive' on the bottom right, and keep finding activities corresponding to each area.

Visitor : I see. This method involves dividing it into four sections and writing down the items for each area. Is that right?

Mentor: That's right. However, it's not easy at first. This process can take several days. It's not something to rush through; it requires careful consideration. If you hastily choose anything, you may lose time and incur financial losses. I remember struggling to find even one item for several days at first. Don't focus solely on one area; try to evenly explore each area and select at least 2-3 substantial items. Also, this is not a one-time task but something you will continue to work on even after retirement. It may be subject to modifications or interruptions along the way. Just completing this much will make a noticeable difference in the quality of life compared to retiring without any plans.

Visitor : So, should I divide it into four sections and write down the items for each area? Is that enough?

Mentor: No, that's not enough. As I mentioned, just thinking about the activities each person should pursue in each area can make a big difference, but that alone doesn't complete the process. Therefore, you should prepare a notebook to jot down specific execution methods for each item in each area, and record the considerations on how to proceed with each activity.

Visitor : It's great that you mention the need for a notebook to jot down an execution plan, but now I'm curious about what to research, what to record, and how to do it.

The secret of the WILD rule

Mentor: That's right. It's a very important point. Allow me to share a tip that I personally find useful as a specific execution method. I suggest using the 'WILD rule' for exploring activities in the 'Retirement Preparation 4 Areas.' The WILD rule is an approach that follows the initials of WILD in English.

Visitor : You mentioned to follow the execution method according to the WILD rule. So, specifically, how should I do it?

Mentor: The WILD rule is a method that I find most convenient to use when facing challenges. I will have a separate opportunity to explain it in detail later. For now, I will simply explain the basic steps.

Visitor : You mentioned that you will explain it in detail separately. So, what is the WILD rule in a nutshell?

Mentor: WILD is an acronym where the first letter W stands for 'Wan't, which means you need to identify and desire something intensely. It emphasizes the importance of discovering what you truly want. Most people struggle to identify what they truly desire. I also had difficulty finding what I truly desired at first.

4 steps of WILD challenge

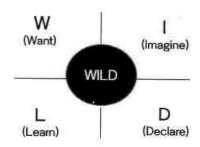

W
(Want)

I
(Imagine)

WILD

L
(Learn)

D
(Declare)

Visitor : So, what did you find?

Mentor: After contemplating what I desired most after retirement, I eventually discovered that it was none other than cooking meals for my family.

Visitor : It seems that cooking meals for your family was what you desired most. So, what was the second 'I'?

Mentor: The second 'I' refers to 'Imagine', which means envisioning. In this case, you need to imagine two things. First, imagine the joyful image of yourself when your desired goal is achieved. The other is to imagine the preparations needed to accomplish that goal. In my case, since cooking meals for my family was my desire, I imagined the satisfaction of completing that task. I wanted to cook delicious meals and receive compliments from my family. The second thing to imagine is how to make it happen. For me, if I wanted to cook for my family, I knew I had to learn how to cook. There are many different ways to learn, such as self-study, attending cooking classes, or even going to a lifelong learning center in the community. I decided to pursue a national certification to ensure that I learned properly. Then I thought about how I would go about obtaining the certification. Ah! I should attend a cooking academy! I needed to figure out which academy, when to attend, how to get there, and how much it would cost. This detailed research phase is important. Once you have a clear direction, determine the feasibility and timeline, record the details in a notebook, and finalize your commitment to pursue one item with actionable steps. This is where the 'Practical Bucket List' comes into play.

Visitor : OK. It goes through these stages to be included in the 'Practical Bucket List'.

Mentor: That's right. The actionable bucket list is a very meaningful tool for me, and I plan to explain it separately.

Visitor : Then, what is the third letter of WILD, which is L?

Mentor: L stands for Learn in WILD. It represents the process of learning, as imagined in 'Imagine' step. This learning is crucial to ensure that all activities become achievable. Most of the activities I undertake take several years or at least 2-3 months, so it is essential not to neglect this aspect. In fact, through this stage, unexpected self-core brands can be created in various places. If you go through this retirement preparation process, you will easily feel why it requires so much time.

Visitor : Learning is indeed very important. So, what does the last letter D stand for?

Mentor: The last letter D stands for 'Declare'. This stage can be considered to take place almost simultaneously with the third stage. Declaration is a crucial element in motivation. There can be various ways to declare, but it's about finding your own way of declaring. Whether it's writing it in a diary, posting it in a family band, or making a verbal promise, you can do it in your own way. However, personally, I record it in the 'Practical Bucket List' I mentioned earlier and attach it in a visible place where anyone can easily see it. For me, it seems like there is no better way than this. Alright! We have finished explaining the detailed design stage of the first step, the retirement preparation in the development of Self-core brand, and now I will continue to explain the second step, the specific execution stage.

Visitor : Your approach of making plans and taking action appears to be very systematic and specific. Now, please go ahead and explain the second step.

Mentor: Before proceeding to the second step, let's briefly review the first step. Step 1 involves the detailed design phase for the four areas of retirement preparation: Sollive, Comlive, Challive, and Vollive. Draw a crossword grid on a blank sheet and fill in each area with corresponding activities. To bring those activities to life, I explained the 'WILD principle,' where W stands for Want, urging to identify your heartfelt desires, I for Imagine, encouraging you to envision the outcome and how to achieve it. The third step, L, emphasizes the importance of learning through actual study to achieve your goals, and finally, D stands for Declare, suggesting that you declare your commitment to implement your plan in your own way. Building upon this foundation, the second step involves the practical implementation of these designed elements within each area.

Visitor : That's right. Having gone through the planning phase of Step 1, it's now time to proceed with the actual implementation.

Mentor: That's right. However, the most crucial point here is something that I emphasize the most during my lectures. It's the English alphabet 'S.' What do you think the letter 'S' represents?

Visitor : The letter 'S'? Well, what is it?

Mentor: Here, the letter 'S' signifies 'Specific.' When it comes to retirement preparation, what I consider most important is to be specific. Simply keeping everything in mind and thinking that it will work out won't lead to concrete implementation. It is crucial to execute things in a specific manner during the implementation phase.

Visitor : Then, in the second step, can you give an example from your case?

Mentor: Most of what I have accomplished has been achieved through this stage. For example, I had a strong desire to write a book on retirement preparation, so I imagined a book-writing method using a Naver Blog. Through this, I started writing a book using a blog. Over a period of about three months, I practiced writing the book on the blog and eventually completed the final book. Another example is when I wanted to develop KakaoTalk emoticons for middle-aged users. I purchased books on emoticon production and started studying. I also studied Photoshop to create each emoticon design, starting from the initial sketches to the final submissions in Photoshop. It took about four months of preparation to submit the finished work. This became a concrete implementation stage in the second step. Another example is when I wanted to learn POP (point of purchase). I purchased books on POP and started learning from the basics. I eventually obtained a certification. Additionally, to create a rap song for my son, I started by watching rap programs like 'Show Me the Money' and 'High School Rapper.' Over a preparation period of about five months, I wrote rap lyrics, received help from a professional rapper to add beats, and completed the final rap. The title of the completed rap song is 'Miracle'. In this way, the second step represents the implementation stage to achieve various goals. The common aspect among them all is that they started with specific actions.

Visitor : Ah! I see. After hearing your explanation, I realize that this stage is going to be very important. Shall we continue to the third step then?

Mentor: OK. Through this process, we move on to the third step. The third step can be considered as a phase of focusing on your areas of interest. In simpler terms, it serves as a stepping stone between the '4 areas of the retirement preparation' and the 'Self-core brand'. As I mentioned before, during the process of developing items in the '4 areas of the retirement preparation' and progressing with specific activities, there will inevitably be activities that capture your strong interest. It is during this stage that you start to concentrate more on those specific items. For example, in the challenge of developing emoticons that I mentioned earlier, if I were to further research and concentrate on this, and continue to engage in artistic activities in the world of emoticon creation, I could work as an emoticon artist and even make it my second job. This concentrated phase is exactly what I'm referring to. Although I failed to join KakaoTalk's emoticon studio despite my long hours and efforts, it is a true story of my striving to become an emoticon artist and also one of my proudest challenges so far. Due to time constraints, I cannot provide explanations for all the other examples, but once I finish explaining the fifth step, I will provide a comprehensive explanation of the areas I focused on.

Visitor : Sure! Let's move on to Step 4 then. You mentioned that Step 4 is the conceptualization phase for differentiation in the chosen field. How can you explain it?

Mentor: Step 4 is the stage where you brainstorm whether it is possible to differentiate yourself in the chosen field after going through Step 3. Let me explain using my own case as an example. In my preparation process, there was an activity that I tried to differentiate myself in, which was the unmanned aerial vehicle called a drone. You may already know that drones are one of the key items in the Fourth Industrial Revolution. I was also interested in this field and started studying drones while reading books related to the Fourth Industrial Revolution. I realized that drones had great potential, so I began studying how they could be practically utilized in the future. This kind of evaluation is crucial. Even if it's a field you're passionate about, if it's not realistically achievable or requires excessive investment, you can't just start without careful consideration. I focused on reading books and searching the internet, and even attended several drone exhibitions to observe and gather more information.

Visitor : Ah, I see. You're taking on a challenge in a new field. So, what were the results of your evaluation?

If it's not the path for me, don't go

Mentor: Based on my evaluation, I have determined that it is worth initially pursuing, so I have decided to move forward with specific execution steps. I have decided to start by setting a goal of obtaining a certification. I purchased books and studied for one month in preparation for the written exam. However, the practical exam is crucial. To prepare for it, I needed to complete a certain number of training hours at a specialized institution and actually take the practical exam. Considering the significant cost and the lack of proximity for learning, I had to find a suitable academy to attend. During the process of assessing whether this field could become my secondary profession, I focused on exploring the use of drones in the agricultural field. I had doubts about how practical it would be in Korea, especially considering the cost of purchasing a drone that would be suitable for the intended purpose. Ultimately, I reached the conclusion that it was not a suitable fit for my Self-core brand, so I decided to fold it. This evaluation can be considered as the fourth stage, the stage of formulating a differentiation strategy. It involves assessing whether the chosen field can offer differentiation. It's important to note that once we start, we don't necessarily have to continue everything indefinitely. Just as it was advised not to go if it's not the right path, it requires wisdom to know when to step back at a certain point.

Vsitor : I see. Now there is only one last stage left, which is the fifth stage.

Mentor: The fifth stage can be considered as the stage where the Self-core brand is created. Once the differentiation plan of the fourth stage is completed and a clear determination is made to proceed, this stage can be seen as the final stage in which the Self-core brand is commercialized and specialized in the field. In other words, this stage is about concretizing the actual activities one wants to pursue and can serve as a stepping stone to a second profession if one desires to develop it into a career.

Visitor : Okay, I see. You have explained the five stages of building a Self-core brand, but could you please summarize it once again?

Mentor: To summarize, building one's own self-core brand is a five-step process. The first stage is to identify activities related to the four areas of retirement preparation. Second, it is the stage of implementing these activities concretely. Third, it is the stage of further focusing on areas of interest. Fourth, it is the stage of conceptualizing how to differentiate oneself. Finally, the fifth step is to commercialize, develop as a business, and specialize, connecting it to a second career path for the future. This becomes one's self-core brand. I would like to convey that the chosen path becomes a valuable future that can be sustained for a long time, rather than just a temporary job.

Visitor : I really appreciate your kind words. I am very curious about how you have built your own Self-core brand. Could you please tell me once?

Mentor: Sure. I guess it would be easier for you to understand if I give you an overall explanation about my Self-core brand. But before going into specific details, are you curious about why I used the concept of 'brand' to describe my post-retirement goals?

Visitor : Certainly. The reason I was so curious about why you used the term "Self-core brand" to describe your ultimate goals is because I wanted to understand the concept behind it. Could you please explain it to me?

Mentor: First, let's examine the literal meaning of the term "brand." A brand is defined as a combination of unique names or symbols used by the producer or seller of a product or service to differentiate it from competitors. Interpreting this in a modern context, a brand refers to various elements that distinctly differentiate one's own products or services from those of other sellers. Just as products or services require a brand that stands out from others, our lives also require a more distinguished self-brand. Especially after retiring, it's essential to establish a unique self-core brand that distinguishes us from others, enabling us to create an extraordinary golden years of life.

Visitor : I see. You mentioned the importance of having a Self-core brand that sets us apart from others after retirement. What kind of Self-core brand should we strive to have?

Mentor: In fact, before retirement, it can be challenging to establish a Self-core brand due to the focus on organizational goal. However, after retirement, we have the chance to discover our true Self-core brand without interference from others.

Yet, there is an important aspect to keep in mind. It is crucial to find something that aligns with our own characteristics. Just like wearing ill-fitting clothes that are either too big, too small, or don't suit our style, a brand that doesn't align with our characteristics lacks sustainability and cannot become a true Self-core brand. Ultimately, to build a solid Self-core brand, it is essential to have a good understanding of our own characteristics.

Visitor : Understanding one's own characteristics is very important. So, how did you create your Self-core brand?

Mentor: At first, there were no set procedures or methods, so there were many trial and errors. First, like I mentioned, I started by thoroughly preparing activities for the four areas of retirement preparation that I explained. As I mentioned earlier, it was not easy to find activities for each area at first. To summarize, for Sollive, I selected and pursued eight activities, including setting up ARTSPACE19, my living space, and obtaining qualifications for a cook and a baker. For Comlive, I developed seven items, such as regular family barbecues called 'Ask the Stars,' categorized by friends, family, and wife. For Challive, which is all about endless challenges, I selected and pursued around ten activities such as creating my own Naver Blog and trying to make emoticons. Lastly, for Vollive, I focused on three tasks, such as making 500 dishes for my wife until I die.

Visitor : I see. You have prepared and carried out so many things.

Mentor: If I prepare this well, it will become a highly differentiated retirement life. I also thought that with such preparation, it would be a solid and well-structured retirement life. These items were changeable and new additions were possible, so gradually new things were filled in. However, naturally, certain areas became more focused on during this process. Gathering them together to create a Self-core brand, I initially considered about seven roles such as conflict management specialist, drone disaster expert, natural fermentation master baker, restaurant startup counselor, emoticon artist, and more.

Visitor : It seems that a lot of fields were considered. So, what did you finally decide on for your Self-core brand?

Mentor: No, it wasn't easy to decide. At the beginning, I had so much enthusiasm that I ended up considering many things. However, many of the areas that were considered were found to be either impractical or difficult to specialize in. Let me explain the drone disaster expert I mentioned earlier in more detail. Initially, the results of this area's consideration were judged to be worth trying out in concrete execution stages, based on my judgment. And during the process of considering whether this area could be my next profession, I focused on the use of drones for agricultural disaster management. In Korea, there were doubts about their usability, and especially after confirming the fact that I would have to purchase a drone that was suitable for the purpose after acquiring a license, I reached the conclusion that it was not suitable for my Self-core brand and decided to fold it. Just because you started something does not mean you have to continue with it. Sometimes it is necessary to stop at a certain point. I am saying this again because if you do not think it is right for you, you should be able to give up boldly. If you cannot stop because of the time and money you have invested so far, you will miss out on even greater things.

Visitor : So, how did you ultimately create your Self-core brand through that?

Writing books, my Self-core brand No.1

Mentor: In my case, my self-core brand was created quite accidentally. It's truly a fascinating story. While pursuing my goal of 'My Blog at the age of 60', which I mentioned earlier, I decided to gather all the retirement preparation content I had been working on for each category. With all the prepared content put together, it turned into a real book. That's when I made the decision to become a retirement preparation specialist writer and went through the process of publishing the book. I decided to title the book, Eun-jun-in which means retirement planner. That's how I truly became a retirement preparation specialist writer. Afterward, I wrote another book related to retirement preparation. The title of my second retirement-related book is 'Succeeding as a Baecksoo After Retirement'. This became my first Self-core brand.

Visitor : OK. You wrote a book about retirement preparation and became a retirement preparation specialist writer. If this became your first Self-core brand, do you have any other Self-core brands?

Mentor: Let me explain. I ended up creating one Self-core brand in a very unexpected way. After writing the book, I started receiving requests for lectures on the topic. That's when it hit me. I realized I could develop this into a professional career, so I followed the process of creating a Self-core brand by specializing in each aspect. First, I created lecture materials and made informational pamphlets to send out to various places. As a result, I received more requests for lectures from different places. Unexpectedly, I also started receiving requests to give lectures to corporate employees, government officials, and the college students. This led me to establish a second career as a retirement preparation lecturer.

Visitor : Ah, I see. Yes, I heard that you also give lectures in various fields other than retirement preparation.

Mentor: That's right. At first, I was only giving lectures in the retirement field, but I realized that lecturing was a perfect fit for my personality. So, I decided to venture into other fields. I had a keen interest in the safety field, so I made up my mind to obtain certifications related to safety. I started with the Safety Management Supervisor certification and went on to acquire four more certifications: Disaster Safety Supervisor, Children's Safety Supervisor, Silver Safety Supervisor, and Psychological Safety Supervisor. With these five safety certifications, I am now actively working as a safety specialist instructor and lecturer. Building upon this foundation, I applied to become a civil defense education instructor organized by the local government, and I became a civil defense education instructor. This allowed my second Self-core brand, the

'Becoming an Instructor' project, to gain more recognition and establish its place.

Visitor : That's truly amazing. It seems like the possibilities are endless. Do you lecture in any other fields besides this one?

Mentor: Yes, as I continued with lectures like this, I unexpectedly started lecturing in various other fields. I taught at the Lifelong Learning Center, the Senior Lifelong Education University, and the Senior citizen college. And I also acquired a 1st-grade interviewer certification and conducted job-seeking lectures for job seekers, and now I am working as a 1:1 interview mentor. Despite all these preparations, I have experienced the pain of many lectures and schedules being cancelled due to the unexpected setback of COVID-19, but the role of lecturer has become my own sturdy 'Self-core brand'.

Visitor : Yes, that's right. I've been able to hear various stories from you about the process of building a Self-core brand after retirement. It seems that utilizing practical tools like this can have a significant impact. However, I imagine you faced many challenges in the beginning, didn't you?

Curious about my future in 5 Years

Mentor: Yes, that's correct. It was challenging. As I mentioned, I didn't start with the four areas of retirement preparation and the Self-core brand tool from the beginning. Instead, I developed these tools while going through the retirement preparation process myself, which brought many difficulties. At this point, I can confidently say that anyone can have a successful retirement preparation by using this practical tool I've developed. Even though retirement may not be closely related to you, if you truly desire a better life, following this approach step by step can lead to a life that is completely transformed. I have the conviction that this is possible because I am the one who has experienced it firsthand. As I who had no plans after retirement, I'm now enjoying a retirement lifestyle that I couldn't have anticipated just a few years ago. And what's more important is that this is not the final stage, but still just the beginning. In fact, I am very curious myself. I wonder what I will be like in one year, in five years, in ten years, even in twenty years. My challenges through this method will continue because challenges always leave a lasting impact.

Visitor : I see. You are truly enjoying a satisfying retirement life. It feels even more real to me after meeting you here today and hearing about your journey. However, I imagine you must have faced various challenges along the way. I would like to discuss that aspect this time. What kind of difficulties did you encounter?

7

The challenge pays off
in the end.

Mentor: As I explained earlier, while pursuing my own Naver blog at the age of 60, I wrote my first book. Based on this, I became the first 'ARTCOACH' title holder and a retirement specialist instructor, traveling to various places. I went further by obtaining five safety certifications in the safety field to become a safety specialist instructor, which led me to venture into various fields as an instructor, including civil defense. I thought that by lecturing in various fields like this, I could live a proper and exemplary life in my golden years of my life. However, I faced an unexpected setback.

Visitor : You have prepared quite well, but what is an unexpected setback?

The unexpected setback

Mentor: It was truly an unexpected event. It was the emergence of COVID-19. This virus, which I thought would end soon, continued for a long time and caused great difficulties for many people. It also caused me great pain. All 70 lectures scheduled for the first half of the year after my retirement were canceled, which made me sit alone in an empty office. As a result, I was slowly getting exhausted, both physically and mentally.

Visitor : COVID-19 has indeed presented formidable obstacles for you. How did you manage to overcome them?

Mentor: At first, I went through an incredibly challenging time. There were many people who were facing more difficulties than I was, so as I had to endure in silence, it was not easy to handle. Because I had prepared a lot and had high expectations up until this point. However, I suddenly thought that I couldn't spend this time so meaninglessly. So, a challenge for something new began to stir in my heart. That's why I decided to challenge myself in a new area. Through these challenges, COVID-19 gave me two unexpected and significant gifts.

Visitor : Did COVID-19 give you unexpected gifts?

Became a YouTuber with a 2M Views

Mentor: Yes, COVID-19 gave me a gift. Not just one, but two. The first gift is becoming a YouTuber.

Visitor : You're saying being a YouTuber is a gift from COVID-19?

Mentor: Yes, it's true. It would have been something I almost couldn't have done if it weren't for COVID-19. Learning YouTube on my own at the age of over 60 wasn't exactly easy, but during the social distancing period caused by COVID-19, I took advantage of the time and spent about 4-5 months progressing in my studies on YouTube. I realized that the concepts were not as difficult as I had initially thought. I purchased the necessary equipment, went through the process of creating and uploading actual videos, and focused on extracting the key points that would make it easier for middle-aged individuals like myself to learn YouTube. I recorded and uploaded a 17-lesson YouTube video lecture series. In particular, I created something called a 'YouTube Map,' the first of its kind in Korea, to help anyone easily understand the entire process of YouTube. Through this process, I became a YouTube instructor and now I offer a YouTube lecture series that teaches 'Anyone, regardless of age, can become a YouTuber'.

Visitor : It seems that you became a YouTuber and even started giving YouTube lectures by utilizing the spare time due to the cancellation of lectures caused by COVID-19.

Mentor: That's right. Becoming a YouTuber was listed as the 28th item on my 'Practical Bucket List', and it was actually the most challenging goal for me to pursue. However, COVID-19 gave me the opportunity and courage to have the spare time to pursue it.

Visitor : Wow! So you became a YouTuber because of COVID-19. That's impressive. It must not have been easy for you to take on this challenge at the age of over 60. So, what is the YouTube channel you are currently running?

Mentor: The YouTube channel is operated under the name 'Eun-jun-in TV', which is derived from the title of my book. Currently, there are over 300 videos uploaded. As I have been consistently working on it for several years, the total number of subscribers has exceeded 10,000. Although I am not yet a top YouTuber, I upload videos showcasing my various challenges after retirement. I also have a video that has garnered around 2 million views. Additionally, I receive advertising revenue in dollars from Google, although there may be some monthly fluctuations. It was truly amazing when I received the first deposit of dollars into my foreign exchange account. It made me feel like a patriot to earn foreign currency. With all of this, I can confidently say that I have established myself as a 'Self-core brand' as a YouTuber. I consider COVID-19 to have given me a truly precious gift.

Visitor : Ok. I see. You've overcome the difficulties caused by

COVID-19 after retirement and established yourself as a YouTuber, which is impressive considering your age. Earlier, you mentioned that COVID-19 gave you two big gifts. So what is the other gift?

Mentor: Yes, the other gift that COVID-19 gave me is becoming a lyricist. With the increased time spent sitting at my desk due to the pandemic, I took the opportunity to pursue my long-held desire to become a lyricist.

The second gift of COVID-19

Visitor : While becoming a lyricist is not an easy choice, do you have any special motivation for pursuing it?

Mentor: After working for 35 years in a public corporation, I retired and livrd in Gyeongju. Although it's not my birthplace, it feels like my hometown. It's a place where I worked for a long time, and it's also my wife's hometown. After retiring, while searching for the most fulfilling endeavor in Gyeongju, I realized that there was no representative song that anyone in Gyeongju could easily sing. So, I made up my mind to create a song that would represent Gyeongju. After extensive preparation, I wrote the lyrics for a song called 'Gyeongju Arirang' and found hidden composers and vocalists in the Gyeongju area to complete the song. It took about a year for the planning and the final single album to be released. Now, the song is gradually becoming the representative song of Gyeongju. It is being performed at various events and concerts, including the Gyeongju Arts Center. Especially on June 8th, which is Citizen's Day in Gyeongju, the song was sung as the main song at the event called 'Citizen's Day', where many Gyeongju citizens gather. I feel that now it has truly become the representative song of Gyeongju. This is perhaps the biggest motivation for me to debut as a lyricist.

Visitor : I also went to Gyeongju with my family last time and heard a song called 'Gyeongju Arirang' at an event. So you wrote the lyrics for that song. So you have become a lyricist who is also a part of your Self-core brand, right?

Mentor: Yes, that's correct. As a professional lyricist, I have now embarked on my full-fledged lyric-writing career. So far, I have released five single albums. Apart from 'Gyeongju

Arirang,' my first self-composed lyric, dedicated to my wife, is called 'My Wife Inside Me.' There's also 'a hole sky,' which expresses the pain of separation. Furthermore, I have a song titled 'More Than Audrey Hepburn,' inspired by my lifelong admiration for Audrey Hepburn since childhood. And even amidst the frustrations of the COVID-19 era, a song called 'Brown Mask' has been released, which sings about the encounters with beautiful women. These songs are currently available as music releases. Additionally, I am preparing around ten other songs, including 'Love is Pythagorean Theorem,' to be introduced to the world.

Visitor : The news is that you've already written lyrics for 5 songs and released them as music. It's truly amazing! It seems like you're embarking on a promising path as a professional lyricist. Recently, I came across an online article stating that you received an award in a lyricist competition. Could you tell me more about it?

Mentor: I received the grand prize in a lyrics contest hosted by the media. My winning piece was titled 'Yegiso'. This award holds a lot of meaning for me as a debut lyricist. I hope 'Yegiso' will eventually become a great piece of music by meeting a talented composer and singer.

Visitor : Congratulations, that's a truly meaningful award. By the way, have you made any profit from selling the music? Also, it seems like you really enjoy music, do you do anything else related to music besides writing lyrics?

Mentor: I am currently registered as a member of the Korea Music Copyright Association. Although the amount is still small, I receive monthly earnings from the release of my music. It's fascinating that I can generate income from music. Apart from writing lyrics, I handle the release of the music, including reaching out to music distributors and personally creating the album artwork. I also produce the music videos for the songs myself, without outsourcing. Additionally, if given the opportunity, I have a dream of organizing an audition competition to discover aspiring singers from my place of Gyeongju and provide them with the songs I have produced.

Visitor : It's truly an endless journey of challenges. I admire your attitude of embracing even the challenges brought by the pandemic. It's impressive to see you embodying the spirit of 'Challive' as you mentioned. So, besides that, do you have any other 'Self-core brand' that you would like to pursue in the future?

Mentor: I apologize if it seems like I'm boasting, but I recently published a poetry book. It was a dream I had for a long time, and it has finally come to fruition. It is currently selling well through online bookstores.

At that moment, he stood up from his seat and walked towards the bookshelf. He brought back a small-sized poetry book and, along with a simple message, personally signed it before handing it to the visitor. The message read, "To: Visitor! I offer this book with heartfelt gratitude. May you soon achieve success and become the protagonist of a classy second half of life. - from Eun-jun-in."

Visitor : OK. You mentioned that you published a poetry book. Does that mean you have become a poet now?

Mentor: I'm not a poet, but I'm starting cautiously. When I looked back on the time after retirement, I realized how quickly the years had passed. So, in my free time after retirement, I began jotting down short writings in a notebook. Then, by chance, someone who saw my notebook suggested turning it into a poetry collection. After hesitating, I selected around 100 pieces of writing related to my wife and decided to publish a poetry collection dedicated to her.

Visitor : It's about your wife, and the title is 'Life Shorts'. Does it have a special meaning?

Mentor: Rather than having a special meaning, it's more about the brevity of life. As life is short, the idea behind the title 'Life Shorts' is to express our lives in a concise manner, suggesting that writings should also be short. Just as there are shorts in Youtube, there should be short poems in poetry to create a sense of intimacy. It's a title that reflects the current trend. I recommend categorizing this type of poetry as 'Life Shorts Poems' or 'Living Shorts Poems'.

Visitor : Well, do you have any special intention behind this poetry collection?

Mentor: Rather than a specific intention, it's a collection of episodes with my wife. However, if I were to attribute meaning to it, I belong to the typical Baby Boomer generation. Through my wife, I depict the ambiguous life of a husband in this generation. Additionally, I would like to mention that this poetry collection was not published through a general publishing company, but rather I used a self-publishing platform called 'BOOKK,' which is a startup in the publishing industry. I created the book by using Print-on-demand (POD) ordering, which did not require any upfront costs.

Visitor : What is the POD publishing model?

Mentor: The POD (Print-on-Demand) publishing model works by manually entering and editing the manuscript in the given format, submitting it to the platform for approval, and then waiting. When an order is placed, the printing is done and the ordered book is delivered. This allows anyone with a manuscript to easily have their own book. Isn't it a great idea?

Visitor : That's a great idea indeed. It makes me want to write a book out of the blue as well. You've given me such valuable information. Thank you!

Mentor: Anyone can do it. I've explained the method I used to publish my poetry book on my YouTube channel in detail, so if you refer to it, you can easily follow along.

Visitor : Today, I'm learning a lot and gaining valuable information. Well then, why don't you summarize your Self-core brand for me overall?

Mentor: Sure! Let me summarize it briefly for you. I retired not too long ago, and I now believe that my previous job title during my active career holds no significance. The title I have created for myself after retirement is my 'Self-core brand'. It has become my second career, one that I can sustain for a long time in my life. I started as a writer and now work as a professional instructor in retirement, safety, civil defense, and senior education fields. I also serve as a interviewer and interview mentor for job seekers.

Additionally, I am active as a YouTuber. I have made my debut as a lyricist and am calmly walking the path of a poet. I also spend time writing other books continuously. All of these endeavors I am currently pursuing make up my present title and 'Self-core brand'. I consider them valuable gifts that I never could have imagined in the past. I believe that anyone, just like I did, can create their own 'Self-core brand' step by step and build a successful golden age of life. Assisting with that is my role and my wish.

Visitor : So far, you have explained to me in detail about the four areas of retirement preparation and the creation of 'Self-core brand', including examples. It's truly great that you were able to achieve all of this in just a few years. I also want to learn your determination and productivity. From what I've heard, you will be giving a special lecture titled 'I Almost Became Jobless After Retiring.' Could you please explain what it primarily covers? It would be really helpful for me to have a better understanding of the overall content.

Almost became jobless after retiring

Mentor: In preparation for retirement, when I conduct lectures in the form of special lectures, I usually title it as 'I Almost Became Jobless After Retiring'. The reason behind this is that to discuss practical strategies for retirement preparation, I need to share my own experience. Moreover, I truly believe that if I hadn't prepared in that way, I would have actually ended up being unemployed. Therefore, when I give lectures with that title, I usually divide them into four parts for explanation.

Visitor : You mentioned that you divide the explanation into four parts. I'm Interested about how you divide the explanation into these four parts.

Mentor: First, in Part 1 Introduction, we will provide an explanation of what retirement means to us with the subtitle "Will we become Retirement Preparers or Retirement Recluses?" Then, in Part 2, I will cover the content of the "Four Areas of Retirement Preparation." I will explain the concept of the four areas and delve into each area with specific case examples. Part 3 will discuss our ultimate goal of 'Creating a Self-core 'Brand'. and finally, in Part 4, I will deliver content related to motivation with the title 'Challenges Always Lead to Profitable Business'.

Visitor : When there is an opportunity, I really want to listen to your lecture once. Could you give me a brief summary of the lecture content?

Mentor: Let me briefly summarize it for you. I will first explain the concepts of retirement and post-retirement. We often use these terms interchangeably or tend to use the concept of retirement more broadly, but it seems necessary to clarify them a bit.

Visitor : Well, there seems to be a slight difference. How do you distinguish between the two?

Mentor: If we first examine the meaning of the Chinese characters, we can distinguish the meaning between retirement and post-retirement. Retirement means stepping down from a position or title, which includes the meaning of completing a task or ending something. In contrast, post-retirement means to withdraw and hide for a while, which implies taking a break. However, unlike retirement, the word post-retirement also includes the meaning of a new beginning. This means that retiring leads to a new phase of life, which should be viewed as a separate meaning. However, we tend not to distinguish between the two. That could be because in both cases of retirement and post-retirement, the Korean term is translated as 'retirement' in English.

Visitor : OK. I see. But how would you define the concept of retirement? What meaning would you attribute to it?

Mentor: Through the process of discussing post-retirement, I am giving my own interpretation and assigning a new meaning to it. When we look up the concept of post-retirement in a Korean dictionary, it is described as 'stepping down from a position or ceasing social activities and living leisurely.' This aligns with the meaning of the Chinese characters for post-retirement, which implies stepping back from work and taking a rest. This used to be the typical image of our fathers and grandfathers after retirement in the past.

Visitor : That's right. I also witnessed many scenes like that when I was young. It seems that things have changed a lot since then. Please continue with your thoughts.

Mentor: That's right. I also have memories of seeing many elderly people in the neighborhood retire after turning just a little over 50 and wandering around. However, let me try to interpret 'Retirement' in English by breaking down the word. Some people interpret it positively as 're-tire,' which means to replace the tire and run smoothly. But today, I will interpret it a little differently. The suffix '-ment' in Retirement is a suffix that changes the verb in front of it to a noun. This means that the word in front of '-ment' must be a verb. So, the verb meaning of 'tire' is to become exhausted, to consume all, and to become tired. Therefore, Retirement means 'to become tired again, to consume all again, and to become exhausted again.' So, which is more realistic, the meaning of taking a step back and taking a rest, or the meaning of becoming tired again, consuming all again, and becoming exhausted again? I feel that the latter resonates more with me. I think many people will agree with my opinion in reality. So, what I want to say is that we need to seriously consider what we need to do to avoid becoming tired again or consuming all again after retirement.

Visitor : What do you think you should do to prevent retirement life from becoming tiring after retirement?

Mentor: My answer is very simple. It is to prepare for retirement as I have emphasized so far. Only retirement preparation can enable us to spend our retirement life meaningfully without getting tired or exhausted again. I think you can agree with me on this. So, ultimately, only the methodological issue of how to prepare for retirement remains.

Visitor : I see. So, as a method of preparation, it seems to connect with the idea of building a 'Self-core brand' through the 'Retirement Preparation 4 Areas' that we have learned so far.

Mentor: That's right. So, in the introduction part of my actual lecture, I approach it from various angles, mainly based on statistical data that I have been researching. Especially in the case of Korea, the retirement preparation index, which indicates how well prepared people are for retirement, is much lower compared to other countries. The statistical result shows that the cause is not financial or health issues, but personal activity and human relationships. Therefore, ultimately, the approach that can increase these two areas is needed. In the end, the solution to this is to become a 'Retirement Preparer(Eun-jun-in)', who prepares for the retirement preparation 4 areas.

Visitor : I see. Everything seems to be connected in its own way. That's why the word 'Eun-jun-in' was born.

Mentor: That's correct. We often say that we are living in the era of 100-year life expectancy. However, I believe that we still have to wait a little longer for the actual era of 100-year life expectancy. If we look at the recently announced life expectancy in Korea, it is around 86.1 years for women and 80.3 years for men. By the year 2067, it is projected that women will live beyond 90 years, around 91.7 years, and men will live around 88.5 years. So, it seems a bit difficult to consider it as the era of 100-year life expectancy just yet. That's why instead of the era of 100-year life expectancy, I express it as the 'Triple 30' era, which means living in a cycle where 30 years repeat three times. In other words, Triple 30 divides the 30-year cycle into three stages: the Independent Preparation Stage for the first 30 years, the Economic Activity Stage until the age of 60, and the Golden Age of Life until the age of 90. Just as one needs to be well-prepared as a job seeker in the first stage of independent preparation to succeed in the crucial second stage of economic activity, it is also important to be well-prepared for retirement in the second stage in order to make the most of our third stage, which is our second life. This is the essence of the retirement preparation practical guidebook, the 'Eun-jun-in'.

Visitor : I see. So the process of preparing in this way is called the '4 areas of retirement preparation', right?

A hermit and a retirement preparer

Mentor: That's correct. Ultimately, if you prepare well for retirement, you become a retirement preparer. If you're not well-prepared, you gradually become a hermit. In other words, there's just a small step that separates a hermit from a retirement preparer. That's why specific preparation methods are necessary, and I'm here to introduce the content I have developed through practical implementation. The method I have developed is just one example, and if you have a more systematic and specific method to follow, you can do that. However, the reason I emphasize the 4 areas of retirement preparation is 'balance'. After retirement, you can quickly choose to do what you want. But what's important is that life after retirement should have balance. Didn't we say that the retirement index in our country is poor because personal activities and human relationships are low? If there is no balance in these aspects of life, even if you quickly find a second occupation after retirement, you won't be able to live a fulfilling life. That's why you need to develop areas like Sollive, where you can enjoy yourself even when alone, Comlive, where you can have good relationships with your spouse, family, and friends, Challive, where you continue to challenge and learn, and Vollive, where you can have a more refined life. Specific preparations in these areas are necessary.

Visitor : So, in such a balanced life, it would be a suggestion to develop a Self-core brand. right?

Mentor: Yes, that's right. Now you can give lectures on my behalf. That's exactly it. It's not just about finding a job or starting a business haphazardly, but rather going through a process of striving to balance life and seriously contemplating and developing things that truly align with oneself, even if it's not perfect. Let's create a Self-core brand. That becomes a second occupation that can be sustained for a long time, and even if it's not a profession, it can become a Self-core brand that one wants to pursue.

Visitor : Now that many aspects are understood, what topic would you like to discuss next?

Mentor: Let's delve into the topic of practical motivation for pursuing challenges, focusing on the content mentioned in the final part of my book 'Eun-Jun-in'.

Visitor : You mentioned that we will focus on discussing motivation related to pursuing challenges, right?

Mentor: That's correct. So far, we have discussed dedicating a significant amount of time to the 4 areas of retirement preparation and developing a Self-core brand for a better life. To pursue these new challenges more effectively, motivation is essential for everyone. Therefore, I would like to talk about this aspect.

Visitor : You mentioned the need for motivation for new challenges. So, how can you explain the factors that provide motivation?

Mentor: Generally, motivation is a crucial aspect that addresses the dissatisfaction or deficiency of desires arising from the gap between individual expectations and the reality of the situation. When we analyze the actual forms of motivation, we can identify two main factors: intrinsic factors and extrinsic factors. Extrinsic factors include status, competition, fear of failure, rewards such as recognition or monetary compensation, and so on. On the other hand, intrinsic factors include autonomy, mastery, curiosity, love, and other similar aspects. According to experts' analysis, the most effective factor among these is 'autonomy'.

Visitor : So, it was mentioned that autonomy needs to be increased to provide motivation for challenges. How do you increase autonomy, and what methods do you use?

Motivation follows 'SAD Principle'

Mentor: As a means to ensure autonomy in motivation, I emphasize the MSS(Motivation Self System). The approach I'm suggesting is what I call the 'SAD Principle,' which means making something sad.

Visitor : OK. You mentioned the 'SAD Principle' as a method for self-motivation, which seems to be an acronym using the initials in English. Could you explain what this means in more detail?

Mentor: The SAD Principle is an acronym using the English initials S, A, and D, each with its own meaning. The core of this principle is not relying heavily on external motivation and instead fostering self-motivation autonomously. It can be seen as a type of tool or framework that helps stimulate intrinsic motivation.

Visitor : So, how can we specifically define the SAD Principle? It might feel a bit challenging with the use of acronyms.

Mentor: Not all principles that involve acronyms are difficult. I can say that what I've explained so far is a summary. First, the 'S' in SAD stands for 'Specialized', which means to specialize in the goals one wants to pursue. For example, if someone wants to learn a musical instrument, they should specify which instrument, at what skill level, and in what manner they will learn, and specialize in the concrete methods of execution.

Visitor : First, S stands for Specialized, meaning to specialize. So, what does the second A in SAD stand for?

Mentor: The second A stands for Activity. It means to turn the desired pursuit into a specific set of actions. In other words, if we take learning a musical instrument as an example, while S in Specialized would involve selecting a specific instrument and deciding how to learn it, A refers to creating a specific action goal, or an activity. To help illustrate this, let's consider my own case. For learning a musical instrument, in the first stage of the SAD framework, I chose the shoulder keyboard as the instrument. As for the practice method, I decided to practice consistently for 30 minutes a day through self-study. In the next stage, the Activity stage, my activity goal would be to polish 10 songs on the shoulder keyboard and hold a small recital for my family. This is how you establish specific goals during the activity selection stage.

SAD Principle for MSS

Visitor : Ah, now I understand. So, A in Activity represents specific challenging goals. It seems like you play a unique instrument called the shoulder keyboard. It's impressive that you have a dream of polishing 10 songs and holding a recital for your family. Now, what does the final D in SAD stand for?

Mentor: I already explained what D stands for. It means Declare, which refers to the act of declaring or announcing a goal. This is a crucial step in achieving any goal, as it helps to motivate and drive oneself towards success. It can be seen as a secret weapon that helps to generate self-motivation and keep oneself accountable towards achieving the set goal.

Visitor : I see. So, D stands for Declare, which means to announce or declare a goal. How can we declare our goals effectively? What is your method for declaring your goals?

Mentor: I understand. I mentioned earlier that there are no specific rules for declaring. You can choose any method that suits you. You can say it out loud, write it in your personal journal, or share it with your family and friends. It's up to you to decide the most effective method. However, as for myself, I mentioned earlier that I would provide more detailed information about the operation of my 'Practical Bucket List'. That's what I will explain now.

Practical Bucket List

Visitor : I see. It seems that you have emphasized that part several times. Could you please elaborate more on the Practical Bucket List?

Mentor: Generally, when we talk about a bucket list, we mean writing down the things we desperately want to do before we die. However, I define it as a 'memo-type bucket list'. I participated in a retirement program offered by the company before I retired, and they recommended writing down a bucket list as a regular menu item, but I didn't have much to write and forgot it quickly. What I'm saying is that we need an 'Practical Bucket List' that we can personally accomplish. In fact, this Practical Bucket List is a very important part for me because it plays a role as an intermediate stepping stone between the '4 areas of retirement preparation' we have been promoting and the ultimate goal of creating a 'Self-core brand'. In other words, it is about recording and managing the core activities developed in the preparation process for the four retirement areas in this Practical Bucket List and finding the Self-core brand in that process.

Visitor : I see. So, what do you write on this Practical Bucket List, and how do you manage and operate it?

Mentor: I write down everything I aspire to, want to pursue, and must accomplish on my Practical Bucket List. I turn them into activities and number them on a calendar-sized piece of paper. I keep recording them continuously. To make it easily visible to everyone, I attach it to the most noticeable wall in my living space. I have been operating it this way and find it to be very effective. I plan to continue managing it even after retirement.

Visitor : I see. Then, I am incredibly curious to know what goals are listed on your Practical Bucket List. Could you share them with me?

Mentor: Yes, of course. I'll be happy to share.

He suddenly stood up from his seat, went to the desk, and took a calendar-sized piece of paper attached to the wall above his P.C. He showed it to the visitor. There were many boxes, each with something written, and some had square stamps. He continued his explanation.

Mentor: This is the my Practical Bucket List I mentioned. There are about 75 items listed here. The front pages are all filled, and it continues to the back pages. I started writing it after retirement, and it has already reached about 75 items. Starting from that, as of today, there are about 75 items recorded. Some of them include making a rap for my twin sons, obtaining a national baking certification and starting a home bakery, creating my own living space after retirement, writing a practical guidebook for retirement, becoming a professional lyricist and releasing 10 albums, and reaching the point of generating income as a YouTuber, among others. Out of a total of 75 goals as of today, 48 have been completed, and 27 are currently in progress.

Visitor : Wow! That's amazing. You've already completed 48 items, and you're still working on 27 others.

Mentor: That's right. However, some of them may turn out to be impossible during the process, and plans may be revised or changed, and new things will continue to be added in the future. Ultimately, the process of pursuing each item on my Practical Bucket List is where my self-core brand is developed. In the end, it becomes a milestone that constantly advances my life after retirement.

Visitor : Now I see everything clearly. I think the Practical Bucket List can be a very important tool in developing the self-core brand.

Mentor: Alright! I have explained the content based on my book, 'Eun-jun-in'. That concludes the first day of the lecture. Thank you for listening attentively. I appreciate your dedication in coming all the way and listening until the end. Thank you once again.

Visitor : What are you talking about? I should be the one thanking you. I'm so touched by your passionate explanation. I feel so much and my heart is overwhelmed right now. The process of preparing for retirement in the four areas and developing a self-core brand truly feels like a crucial journey for all of us.

Mentor: One more thing I want to say is that the 4 areas of retirement preparation and the development of a Self-core brand mentioned in my book 'Eun-jun-in' is not just for those planning to retire, but it can be applied to anyone. I want to encourage anyone who is interested to apply this simple method and create a better and more fulfilling life.

Visitor : I can totally relate. I also want to spread this information to many people. But may I ask what content you will be lecturing on tomorrow? Is it okay to ask?

Mentor: I will be covering a slightly different topic tomorrow. In addition to the methodological aspects of retirement, I want to focus on how to cultivate a positive mindset. I plan to conduct the lecture in a conversational format through question and answer sessions. Tonight, please rest here well tonight. I have prepared a bedroom here for you. I will go back to my house to sleep and I'll come back tomorrow morning., By the way, I do a morning walking exercise every day. If you'd like, you can join me as well.

Visitor : Of course! If you allow me to, I'd love to join you for the morning exercise. Let's do it together!

Mentor: Okay, then I'll see you at 7 a.m. tomorrow morning. Sleep well, and see you tomorrow!

Visitor : Yes, please sleep well too. Thank you so much for today.

8

Escape from jobless 'Baeksu'

For the morning workout, the mentor took the visitor to a very beautiful and large lake called Bomun Lake. They parked their car near the lake and after a light stretching session, the two of them walked around the Bomun Lake at a brisk pace. It was actually the visitor's first time walking around Bomun Lake. Even though it was early in the morning, there were quite a few people out exercising around the lake. The visitor couldn't help but think that he had been foolishly using the treadmill at the apartment gym every day. Walking with nature and breathing with nature felt like real exercise.

After finishing their workout, they went to a spa sauna located in a building adjacent to a hotel near Bomun Lake. It wasn't too expensive, but the interior was magnificent. They stayed at a place equipped with a large enough tub to swim in and even an outdoor bath. They chatted away while enjoying the facilities. The visitor sighed, wondering why he had been living such a busy life, and the mentor joked that he wasn't much different himself.

After the sauna, the two of them headed to a sundubu-jjigae (soft tofu stew) restaurant. The mentor pointed out that when you mention Bomun Lake, you have to mention sundubu-jjigae. Among the various side dishes, the restaurant he ate at left a lasting impression as the best restaurant in the visitor's life, with a thumbs-up gesture in his mind. After the meal, they returned to the hideout named 'ARTSPACE19'.

Visitor : You gave me so much guidance yesterday, and this morning you've given me a bundle of gifts including exercise, sauna, a delicious meal, and wonderful memories. I am truly grateful for the precious time you've created. Moreover, I can't forget the taste of the garlic steak you made for me yesterday. I will forever be your student and repay you.

Mentor: I simply share what I have started a little earlier. We are companions on the ship called 'Eun-jun-in'. My dream is for many retirees to no longer fear retirement, to prepare well in the 4 areas of retirement preparation, and to create a wonderful Self-core brand, living the golden years of life splendidly as Eun-jun-in. That's all I hope for.

Visitor : Anyway, thank you so much. So, what kind of class are you going to teach today?

Mentor: Today, I would like to talk about the mindset or attitude after retirement. To clarify, if yesterday I talked about the technical aspect of how to have a good retirement life, today I want to explain the mental aspect of how to operate those tools effectively. No matter how good the tool we have, I think it all depends on the retiree's mindset when it comes to how to live a good retirement life. Also, when we actually implement the methods presented yesterday, it can take a lot of time and obstacles can occur, so having the right mindset and attitude is very important.

Visitor : It seems that you're emphasizing the importance of the mental aspect, attitude, and mindset when it comes to retirement life.

Mentor: That's right. Let's think about soccer for a moment. The most essential thing in soccer is individual skills, followed by team tactics to harmonize those skills based on each position. However, no matter how good the individual skills and team tactics are, if the players' individual mental states are not established, the team may not be able to win or become a good team. The same goes for retirement life. Even if we have good tools for retirement, if we don't change our individual lifestyle, attitudes, and so on, we may not achieve good results. That's why today's conversation with me is just as important as yesterday's. Do my words resonate with you?

Visitor : I understand. It seems like today will be another interesting session. Before we dive into the first topic, I have a question. Among your lecture titles, you mentioned a special lecture titled 'I Almost Became 'Jobless Baeksu' After Retirement.' I'm curious to know why you used the term 'Baeksu' and if there's a specific reason behind it.

Mentor: Ah, Baeksu! That special lecture is the most popular among my lectures. Because the word Baeksu is gradually becoming a reality. Baeksu, which is used as a joke in

Korean to refer to someone who doesn't have a job and idles around without purpose, can be associated with English words like idle, jobless, and unemployed. Therefore, if you don't prepare for retirement at all, it's natural to become Baeksu after retirement and potentially even become a hermit, wouldn't you agree? It has been a long-standing issue in Japan. In Japan, such individuals are referred to as 'Hikikomori(ひきこもり)', meaning reclusive loners. In Korea, too, the number of Baeksu has been increasing since about 10 years ago. These trends are becoming increasingly worse, and they can only be considered as a truly serious problem. In this sense, mentioning Baeksu is only natural, and it can also be seen as the ultimate goal of retirees to escape from being Baeksu.

Visitor : Did you say that escaping from jobless 'Baeksu' is the ultimate goal for retirees?

Mentor: Yes, that's right. I always mention jobless Baeksu in my special lectures for retirees. Before diving into the main topic, I use it as an icebreaker to talk about how escaping from jobless Baeksu is the ultimate goal for retirees. It's just a fun way to warm up the audience. Let me share it with you, so give it a listen and enjoy.

Visitor : It sounds really interesting. I'm very curious.

Five types of jobless 'Baeksu'

Mentor: Baeksu is a symbolic term in Korean that encompasses the meanings of unemployment, joblessness, and idleness, representing a person in a state that includes all of these. To emphasize this, I will use the term itself as it is. Then, I divide the **jobless** 'Baeksu' into five types. Among them, I would like to mention three types of Baeksu that should never be followed after retirement, as well as one type that should be considered as a goal. Let's talk about the direction of life after retirement based on this. First, let's examine the five types of **jobless** 'Baeksu' that I find most intriguing. Although there are various classifications for the Baeksu, today I will clarify the types of Baeksu according to my own method. The types of Baeksu can be divided into different levels. We can categorize them into five levels. Among them, the most common type of Baeksu, corresponding to Level 3, is commonly referred to as 'Neighborhood Baeksu'. This refers to someone who mainly spends their time in their neighborhood. Since their neighborhood is where they live, they tend to handle everything within the neighborhood. They usually frequent local restaurants, local supermarkets, and local barbershops. When they are bored, they might take a walk in the neighborhood park before returning home. This is the important routine of a Neighborhood Baeksu.

Visitor : Level 3 is called 'Neighborhood Baeksu,' right?

Mentor: Yes, that's right. 'Neighborhood Baeksu' is all about playing with the kids in the neighborhood who are still around. But even that is not easy these days. There are fewer kids to play with as most of them are busy attending academies, taekwondo studios, or piano lessons. So 'Neighborhood Baeksu' feels even lonelier these days. On the other hand, Level 2, which is one step lower than 'Neighborhood Baeksu,' is called 'Homebody Baeksu'. Homebody Baeksu represents the most typical Baeksu style. They solve all three meals a day at home and rarely go outside. Their favorite hobby is watching TV. They turn on the TV as soon as they wake up and watch TV for more than 15 hours a day, including morning dramas. They know all the news channels and can memorize over 100 of their own channel programs. Some Homebody Baeksu even have wives who still care for them, but there are also Baeksu who have been completely given up on by their wives.

Visitor : There are Baeksu who have been completely given up on by their wives. Really?

Mentor: Yes, that's right. There are Baeksu who spend their days without showering, indulging in alcohol and lying around in the room. They are in a state where their wives can no longer tolerate them, and they are called 'Hopeless

Baeksu'. It means a jobless person without hope, even abandoned by their wives. This Hopeless Baeksu can be considered as the lowest level of Baeksu, level 1. They can be seen as the prime candidates for twilight divorces. These 'Hopeless Baeksu' are truly in an irreparable state, and there are more of them around us than we think. We can also classify Homebody Baeksu and Hopeless Baeksu as hermits. People who have withdrawn from social life and live in seclusion are called "Hikikomori" in Japan, as I mentioned earlier. Hikikomori is often described as a recluse or a social isolate. I keep emphasizing this because it is a fact that there are many of them around us. Anyone can easily become like that. Now that we have looked at the levels 1, 2, and 3 of Baeksu, let me explain level 4, which represents a slightly different aspect of Baeksu.

5 levels of 'Baeksu'

Level 1 Hopeless Baeksu	Level 2 Homebody Baeksu	Level 3 Neighbor-hood Baeksu	Level 3 Glamorous Baeksu	Level 3 Escape Baeksu

Visitor : Are you saying there is a different type of Baeksu?
Mentor: Yes, the Baeksu corresponding to Level 4 is called

'Glamorous Baeksu.' Glamorous Baeksu mainly plays golf for 3 to 4 days a week. On weekdays, they go to the sauna every day and always dress in luxury clothes and shoes. They also travel overseas for golf trips at least once or twice a month, living a truly glamorous life. Even after retirement, there are a few friends who continue to live like that. They are called 'Left-hand Baeksu' as a different term. Because they play golf so often that their left hand turns pale. Glamorous Baeksu could be considered an idol for all retirees. Most retirees try to imitate Glamorous Baeksu's lifestyle after retirement, but it doesn't last long. Based on careful observation, the most likely type to develop into Hopeless Baeksu is Glamorous Baeksu. After spending a few years enjoying themselves with the money they saved during their working years, retirement pay, and pensions, they may temporarily transform into Neighborhood Baeksu, then move from Neighborhood Baeksu to Homebody Baeksu, and eventually become Hopeless Baeksu, being pessimistic and only reminiscing about the good old days when they were doing well. Perhaps it's a natural outcome when they think about the times they neglected their spouse and enjoyed themselves alone. Now, only one Baeksu is left!

Visitor : It's really interesting. So, what is the last Baeksu?

Final stage: Escaped Baeksu

Mentor: The final stage of Baeksu is 'Escaped Baeksu'. This refers to a group that has escaped from Baeksu. In the world of Baeksu, Escaped Baeksu is also referred to as Baeksu's heretics or rebels. It refers to those who break free from the conventional framework of Baeksu and live their golden years through new, refreshing activities. One of the most representative figures of this lifestyle is former US President Jimmy Carter. After retiring, he went back to his hometown, a small community with fewer than 700 residents. He founded the 'Habitat for Humanity' project to build houses for the poor, and has pursued many other wonderful endeavors such as volunteering as an election observer in underdeveloped countries. Although we may not be able to achieve such a life, shouldn't we at least create a retirement life where we can manage and take responsibility for our own lives?

Visitor : To summarize what you said, the final stage of Baeksu is the Escaped Baeksu, which represents the world we should aim for. In a way, it implies breaking free from Baeksu and embracing a world that is different from Baeksu itself.

Mentor: That's correct. I have explained five types of Baeksu so far. The important thing to note here is that the type of

Baeksu is not determined right after retirement. It's only after moving around here and there and reaching the fifth year after retirement that one can accurately determine which type of Baeksu they belong to.

Visitor : In each individual's case, it can be said that the general form of their Baeksu status is roughly determined around the fifth year after retirement.

Mentor: Sure. When we look at the ratio around the fifth year after retirement, Neighborhood Baeksu and Homebody Baeksu account for 30% and 50%, respectively, making up a total of 80%, and even the Hopeless Baeksu accounts for 10%, which means that one out of ten retirees is in a very serious state. In addition, the Glamorous Baeksu, which accounted for 30-40% after retirement, gradually decreases over time and at the fifth year point, it is difficult to maintain even 5%, and the Escaped Baeksu, which is our goal, is also difficult to maintain 5%.

Visitor : So, according to what you're saying, it seems that it's not easy for Escaped Baeksu to maintain 5%.

Mentor: While there may be some variation in the numbers, it is undeniably a matter that resonates enough to be a serious issue. Anyway, if we are to become Escaped Baeksu and escape the Baeksu situation, what should we do?

Visitor : Well, what should we do to escape the Baeksu situation?

Mentor: It's simple. To become Escaped Baeksu and escape the

Baeksu situation, you need to thoroughly prepare for retirement in advance. As I mentioned yesterday, this means preparing for the '4 areas of retirement preparation' and creating a 'Self-core brand' through the process. To summarize again, the 4 areas of retirement preparation are 'Sollive' for preparing for a life that can be enjoyed alone, 'Comlive' for preparing for a life that can be enjoyed together, 'Challive' for preparing for a life of endless challenge and learning, and 'Vollive' for preparing for a life of enjoying serving others. You should prepare for these four areas well and develop the core task discovered in the process into your own 'Self-core brand'. This is the way to become Escaped Baeksu and create a new golden years of our life. Through the path of Escaped Baeksu, I can explain that I am now living a satisfying golden years of my life with six new jobs. However, the important thing is that anyone can do this. I call this 'succeeding as a Baeksu after retirement'. Everyone becomes a Baeksu after retirement, and it's about building things one by one from that state. This ultimately leads to becoming Escaped Baeksu and succeeding as a Baeksu after retirement.

Visitor : I see. Succeeding as a Baeksu after retirement! That's really impressive. I also really want to do the same. I will follow the methods I learned from you this time and definitely join in the journey to become an Escaped

Baeksu and succeed as a Baeksu. Those are really encouraging words. So, what topic would you like to discuss in earnest from now on?

Mentor: This topic is a very interesting story. First, I would like to propose one important word that I want to convey to all retirees.

Visitor : You mentioned it's an important word for all retirees? What is it?

Mentor: The word is 'solitude empowerment'. Let me tell you about this concept of solitude empowerment.

Three powers of Solitude Empowerment

Visitor : Doesn't solitude refer to being alone, lonely, and spending time in solitude?

Mentor: Let me give it a try. The solitude empowerment I'm referring to is very different from loneliness or solitude. It is truly essential after retirement. To cut to the chase, you need to cultivate this solitude empowerment after retirement.

Visitor : You're suggesting to cultivate solitude empowerment after retirement. I'm really want to know now.

Mentor: That's right. You should cultivate solitude empowerment. Especially as you age and retire, it's important to cultivate solitude empowerment more quickly. Because solitude empowerment gives us three remarkable powers.

Visitor : You mentioned three remarkable powers. What are they?

Mentor: You seem to be in a hurry. Let me explain the story slowly. I'll start with the real story of a retired husband. There was once a retired husband who started doing household chores to help his wife, who he had been neglecting. He did the laundry that he couldn't help with before, cooked meals, made side dishes from the market, and even cleaned the house spotlessly from early morning. He even did the dishes after meals. He became a really great husband. His wife was incredibly happy and proudly boasted to her friends that she had the best husband in our country. However, after about six months, she started feeling a sense of loss, as if something had been taken away from her husband. Eventually, she found herself breaking out in cold sweat and feeling suffocated with a racing heart whenever she thought about her husband who was always at home. Her life became lethargic, and she even had trouble digesting food. She even developed depression, thinking that she had lost herself, and eventually came to the decision of divorce, believing that they couldn't live together anymore.

Visitor : You're saying that his wife even considered divorce? That's unbelievable.

Mentor: This is medically referred to as a form of 'Husband Telecommuting Stress Syndrome. In the case of Korea, this symptom typically arises due to a husband's retirement. The important thing is that this is a legitimate illness. From the husband's perspective, it may be difficult to understand. While neither the husband nor the wife is at fault, for a wife who has built her life under the assumption that her husband would not be home for a long time, suddenly having her freedom taken away due to her husband's retirement creates a challenging situation. It is at this point that we can discover a crucial point. As one ages, couples must learn to live together while respecting each other's freedom as a fundamental principle. Respecting each other's freedom means that each person should be able to maintain and sustain their own lives. It may sound repetitive, but I emphasized 'Sollive' as the first area to focus on in retirement preparation among the four areas. This means that solid preparation for a life that can be enjoyed even alone must be in place for everything to come together. In other words, as one gets older, it is necessary to cultivate solitude empowerment for the sake of enjoying life alone through Sollive.

Visitor : What does solitude empowerment specifically mean?

Mentor: In conclusion, solitude empowerment refers to the hidden strength that comes from harnessing the advantages of solitude to the fullest. Here, solitude should be seen as a distinct concept from loneliness. It is by no means about avoiding interaction with others or feeling ignored and isolated. Rather, it is closer to the notion of embarking on a personal path with conviction. Solitude empowerment is about extracting the inherent strengths within solitude and turning them into a powerful essence.

Visitor: Did you say that solitude empowerment is the power derived from extracting only the inherent strengths within solitude? What specifically is that power?

Mentor: Let me tell you. Within solitude empowerment, there lies a very powerful force that we may not have expected at all. It could be a force that has the potential to completely transform our prime years of life. What exactly is the power hidden within solitude empowerment? I would like to share my own understanding of it.

Visitor: I'm extremely intrigued. What kind of power does solitude empowerment possess?

Mentor: Based on my conclusion, I have gained confidence that solitude empowerment can provide us with three amazing powers.

Visitor : What are these three amazing powers exactly?

Mentor: The first is that solitude empowerment provides us with 'maturity'. It may sound a bit difficult, but it means that it helps us to live a properly self-directed life, away from the confusion and indecisiveness of our previous lives. In other words, Solitude Empowerment makes us very mature. So we must proactively increase solitude empowerment by increasing our alone time, also known as loneliness. We must use this time to first understand ourselves. We must reflect on ourselves in a cold and honest way, such as what goals we pursue, what kind of person we are, what we like and dislike, and what we are good at or not. This is the root of living a concrete and mature life. Perhaps this is a power that only solitude empowerment can provide. Based on this, we can live a self-directed life. The first power that solitude empowerment gives us is maturity.

3 Powers of Solitude Empowerment

Visitor: Solitude empowerment helps us become mature and enables us to live proactive lives. I completely agree with that statement. Now, what is the second power?

Mentor: The second power, solitude empowerment, instills in us a sense of 'independence'. Isn't solitude empowerment inherently an independent power? Therefore, by cultivating solitude empowerment, we can avoid wasting unnecessary emotions in our relationships and reduce stress. Naturally, we won't be bound by spouses, family, lovers, or friends, and the best part is that we can understand ourselves properly and define the direction of our lives clearly. Ultimately, it can foster a strong sense of independence. Haven't most of us lived constantly seeking the attention of others? We have endured the stress of challenging human relationships from time to time. All of these pains can always be experienced when independence is not established. By developing solitude empowerment, we can break free from this state and cultivate a strong sense of independence. This can guide those who desire to live a subjective and independent life towards true inner strength. By the way, did you know that this independence makes us even more free?

Visitor : Independence makes us more free? What does that mean?

Mentor: Independence always comes with freedom. Therefore, the greater our sense of independence, the more freedom we have. Solitude empowerment gives us the second power, which is the independence imbued with freedom.

Visitor: So, solitude empowerment cultivates independence, and independence grants freedom. That's what it means. It's fascinating. Now, what is the third power?

Mentor: The third one is truly crucial. I believe that this power of solitude empowerment has guided me in creating my 4 areas of retirement preparation and Self-core brand today. In other words, solitude empowerment awakens the 'creativity' that lies dormant within me. Isn't it amazing? We have lived for so long, missing out on many opportunities, without even securing a special reason or time to unleash our individual creativity. Much of our creativity has been slumbering within us. However, solitude empowerment awakens this dormant creativity within us. We have witnessed many creative works being born in a solitary atmosphere. If we also nurture solitude empowerment, we can live a more creative and innovative life. As we age, this creativity will approach us with even greater energy. Age is not a barrier to creativity. By cultivating solitude empowerment, we can undoubtedly awaken the creativity that lies dormant within us, regardless of our age.

Visitor: Did you awaken the dormant creativity within you with solitude empowerment?

Mentor: Of course. With the solitude empowerment that I have cultivated consistently after retirement, I have accomplished many things in a short period of time. I became a professional writer, a specialist lecturer in retirement preparation, safety, civil defense, and senior-related topics. I became a YouTuber with more than 10,000 subscribers and 200,000 views on my videos. I also made my debut as a lyricist and have been continuously writing lyrics. Additionally, I obtained various new titles such as a Grade 1 interviewer for public institutions and recently published a poetry collection. The solitude empowerment directly gifted me with the motivation to challenge myself in various activities such as playing the drums and shoulder keyboard, cooking, baking, and obtaining over 20 certifications.

Visitor : Are all the things you have accomplished the power of solitude empowerment?

Mentor: That's right. It's the power of solitude empowerment. Without the power, I could never have achieved all those things. Understanding the positive force inherent in solitude, known as solitude empowerment, should now be much easier. However, what's crucial is how you cultivate solitude empowerment.

Visitor: That's right! Even if we want to cultivate solitude empowerment, we may not know how to do it. How can we cultivate solitude empowerment?

Mentor: First, embrace the best strengths inherent in solitude, such as maturity, independence, and creativity, without fearing loneliness. Instead of getting buried in the agony, struggling, and flailing in loneliness, face loneliness head-on and discover the joy of accomplishment and creation within it. You must necessarily transform loneliness into solitude empowerment. Where can you find moments of solitude? Please throw away that kind of fleeting loneliness to a passing dog. My point is to experience the joy of accomplishment and creation in every small challenge. Every day, gradually build up that sense of accomplishment and creation. Ultimately, it comes down to willpower. If you keep trying with that determination, you can easily become acquainted with solitude. I have practiced it myself. One thing is clear: solitude empowerment becomes an important source that can be responsible for our happiness in old age. Those with strong solitude empowerment can also better understand how to live in harmony with others. This is because they can appreciate the preciousness of living in harmony much more deeply. I believe that solitude empowerment is undoubtedly a necessary virtue for us, living in the age of centenarians, for our old age.

Visitor: Solitude empowerment! It's really important. It's not about living alone and feeling lonely. Rather, it's about using the time alone to mature, cultivate the strength to live an independent life, and unleash creativity to achieve great things. People who possess such qualities tend to value others more and excel in building relationships. Would it be summarized as saying that?

Mentor: You have understood my words accurately. Many things in our lives are created through introspection, contemplation, and research done alone, and especially after retirement, such time becomes even more necessary. The power that emerges from solitude, the power of that tremendous core, is what makes solitude empowerment powerful. It is the strength of solitude empowerment to seek and make one's own the power that comes from solitude.

Visitor : Your words resonate deeply within my heart. The fact that you convey firsthand experiences makes it easier for me to comprehend. Until now, I believed that if things didn't go according to plan, it was due to bad luck. However, listening to your words, I realize that it's not about luck, but rather the lack of such creative effort that made it difficult to accomplish my goals. Your words truly touch my heart. I am deeply moved.

Mentor: Thank you very much for understanding it well. Since we're talking about luck, I believe that luck is one of the outcomes derived from this creative effort process. Ultimately, to have luck, you need to awaken it and make it follow you. It's not something that randomly falls from the sky one day; that's definitely not how luck works, in my opinion.

Visitor : Do we need to awaken luck? What does that mean?

Mentor: What I'm saying is that it's not about whether luck exists or not, but rather about whether we awaken it or not. The absence of luck simply means that we haven't awakened our own luck yet. Now, let me tell you about the ways to awaken luck.

Visitor : I'm really looking forward to this topic as well.

Mentor: First, you need to understand a little about luck. Ultimately, luck exists for everyone. It's not about being unlucky because you didn't learn, or being lucky because you're wealthy, or being unlucky because you're from a humble background, or being lucky because you're from an affluent background. Luck is fairly distributed to everyone. However, the biggest drawback of luck is that it's a sleepyhead. That means luck is always dormant within oneself. So, in order to have luck, you need to awaken your dormant self-luck.

Visitor: We need to awaken our self-luck? Then, how do we awaken that luck?

Mentor: I want to teach you the method. This method is based on the book(Kim Do-yoon/Lucky) which I read with great emotion when I studied luck a few years ago. I combined the contents I obtained from the book with my own rules and now I am introducing a practical method that I am actually using after retirement. I always keep this method in mind and act accordingly. Since then, I have been living with the experience of having a lot of luck. I am convinced that this rule is awakening my dormant luck. There is still a lot of dormant luck within me, so I need to awaken the rest of it.

Visitor : I'm intrigued by that rule.

The 7 rules to awaken luck

Mentor: There are a total of seven rules to awaken luck. To simplify the message, I have organized them with one keyword each. By considering the characteristics of the seven categories of people represented by those keywords, it will be easier to remember. I refer to them as '7 Keywords of Good Luck'. The first keyword of the seven rules to awaken the dormant luck within oneself is to keep a Sherpa, who will serve as the navigator of life, close by.

7 keywords of Good Luck

Visitor : Yes, it means the Sherpa that people speak of when they go mountain climbing.

Mentor: That's right. In our lives, it is essential to have a collaborator, like the Sherpas of the Himalayan expedition teams. In other words, it means that ultimately, it is people who bring us luck, and all opportunities for success come from people. It means to meet someone who can serve as a guiding navigator for our own lives. If all human relationships are only connected by friendship, there may be an issue. The person we need to be close to right now is not necessarily someone who makes us comfortable, but rather someone who is doing well in their respective field. This is because successful people often attribute their success to the decisive help they received from someone around them, which became the catalyst for their success. We also need to be close to such people and learn how we can emulate their positive aspects through them. It means making their efforts our own, which is the first rule to awaken the dormant luck within ourselves.

Visitor : It seems like the saying is to keep a collaborator who can help oneself. It means that luck is created through that collaborator. It feels like a very accurate statement. Today, meeting you and learning such valuable teachings is precisely the act of awakening luck. So, what is the second rule?

Mentor: The second keyword of the '7 Keywords of Good Luck', which awaken the luck within me, is learning from skilled surfers.

Visitor : Are you referring to surfers who ride waves in the ocean?

Mentor: That's right. When skilled surfers ride the waves, they always pay close attention to the movement of the waves. In other words, they need to read the movement of the waves well in order to ride them successfully without any mishaps. We are now living in a digital world where everything has become possible through a single mobile device. The pace of change in the world is so fast that it's difficult to keep up by just running and experiencing things firsthand. We need to be able to read the speed of change as fast as it has changed. We are constantly at the crossroads of choices. We are well aware of how important it is to make good choices in this process.

However, in this process of making choices, there are always various difficulties and challenges, just like waves. Even when faced with these challenges, we must never lose the wisdom to look ahead to the next situation. In other words, like a surfer who observes the movement of the waves and quickly gets out of a difficult situation, it is important to look ahead and determine how to move forward, rather than simply blaming the past. This approach is the second method to awaken the luck within me.

Visitor : Like a surfer carefully observes the movement of waves, we should also not simply give up or surrender when faced with difficulties. Instead, we should carefully assess the next situation and navigate forward successfully.

Mentor: Exactly. You catch on very quickly. The third of the '7 Keywords of Good Luck' for awakening the hidden luck within us is to learn from professional golfers who keep the ball on the fairway. Life is not about speed, but about direction. It's because speed comes from having a clear direction. If you don't know where you're heading, you can't just go full speed ahead, can you? This is similar to professional golfers. Even if you hit long shots with a fast head speed, if the ball goes in the wrong direction and goes out of bounds instead of landing on the fairway, the game will be ruined. Similarly, direction is important in life. But the reason direction is more important than speed is ultimately to reach the destination quickly. There isn't much to gain from arriving late. So, what is the way to increase speed while ensuring direction? It's not just about setting clear goals that correspond to the direction, but also about setting detailed goals that can be seen as structuralizing. Achieving detailed goals ultimately leads to the bigger goal. In other words, how about using the analogy of taking a detailed iron shot and chip shot after the driver, and finally the putting? This is the third way to awaken the hidden luck within us.

Visitor : Your words indicate that one way to awaken our luck is by securing directionality while increasing speed, just like professional golfers, and paying attention to the finer details. To do so, we need to make efforts towards achieving specific goals alongside our larger objective. What's the fourth?

Mentor: The fourth of '7 Keywords of Good Luck' that awakens the luck within me is to escape from the perseverance of being a slave to turning the wheel. Most successful people succeeded because they did something that we did not. If we continue to repeat the same thing in the same way like a slave turning the wheel, we will never succeed. Instead of simply envying successful people, we need to actively find something to improve our current situation. If we continue to fail despite trying, we need to boldly change our input. To awaken the luck within us, we need to boldly escape from the destiny's wheel that is turning in our daily lives, that is, the routine that we are stuck in, and continuously seek something new. That is the signal that awakens the luck within us. Do you understand?

Visitor : Sure, of course. It truly feels like an essential habit. Rather than falling into mannerisms, it can be summarized as the need for constant effort to improve and innovate with new things.

Mentor: You really take things in very well. I think I should call you 'Sponge'. The fifth keyword of '7 Keywords of Good Luck' that wakes up the luck that lies within me is learning from the records of chess or baduk players. We often miss the luck and misfortune in our lives because we use the excuse that we are too busy living. However, if we cannot distinguish between luck and misfortune, we may miss the luck that will come in the future, and we may continue to accumulate misfortune. To avoid making such mistakes repeatedly, we need to take a record like a pro chess or baduk player. If we look back on our past selves enough and distinguish between luck and misfortune in that process and always make an effort to maintain positive lucky energy, we may be able to more easily awaken the luck that lies within us. We cannot live another day, but if we can review our day again, it will surely promise a luckier tomorrow.

Visitor : We cannot relive a day, but the saying that we can look back on a day resonates with me so wonderfully. It's like being able to review our days, just like chess or baduk players, and knowing how to distinguish luck amidst it all, living with a positive energy. It's a remarkable saying.

Mentor: The sixth of the '7 Keywords of Good Luck', which awaken the hidden luck within me, is learning from the triathlon athletes who never give up. The triathlon consists of swimming, cycling, and marathon events, performed consecutively without rest, requiring extreme endurance and physical stamina. We're well aware that athletes endure countless pains and hardships, never succumbing to despair or giving up, striving their best to complete the race. Our lives are no different. Anyone can face difficult situations in life. So, what is most important when we encounter such challenging circumstances? Firstly, accepting that we cannot easily solve this situation, and instead of feeling discouraged or disappointed, we should make an effort to become accustomed to the situation and embrace a positive mindset that sees it as a companion in our journey. Professor George Vaillant from Harvard University, who studied human lives for 72 years, focusing on 268 sophomores, mentioned the findings in his book

'The Conditions of Happiness'. Among the seven conditions of happiness, the first condition is called 'mature defense mechanisms', emphasizing the importance of how we handle and overcome challenges.

Visitor: The first condition of happiness is said to be mature defense mechanisms. It may sound unfamiliar.

Mentor: The meaning of 'mature defense mechanisms' is simply a way of coping with difficulties. If one cannot cope with difficulties in a mature way, no one can achieve happiness. This is the result of a long 72-year study. Now, we must say goodbye to the things that are comfortable and familiar to us and thoroughly learn to cope with difficulties in a mature and flexible way when they arise. Through this process, we can awaken the hidden luck within us.

Visitor: It seems that you have emphasized the wisdom of overcoming difficulties without ever being discouraged or giving up. It is indeed important to have the strength to overcome hardships in order to awaken one's luck and find happiness. So, only the seventh one remains now.

Mentor: The seventh and final one, in the 7 principles of awakening the hidden luck within us, called '7 Keywords of Good Luck' is learning from an archer who draws the bow. If the archer wants to hit the target they aim for, they must draw the bow and release the arrow. It signifies the need to initiate action. The minimum requirement to find our luck is simply to start. The moment of starting anything is often accompanied by more fear than excitement. Isn't it said that we should start not because we know how to do everything perfectly, but because we need to start in order to learn how to do it? We should remember that the starting point is as important as the destination. After all, we can't win the lottery without even buying a ticket, right? Now, you must start. That's how you can awaken the hidden luck within you.

Visitor: So you're saying I should start. The story about the last lottery ticket is truly impressive. Whether it's a jackpot or a dud, you have to scratch it to find out. I truly understand the importance of starting.

Mentor: I have talked about the 7 principles of awakening the luck hidden within me, known as the '7 Keywords of Good Luck'. The 7 keywords I mentioned can be summarized as Sherpa, surfer, golfer, slave, chess or baduk player, triathlete, archer. Ultimately, luck comes to those who choose, work hard, and prepare. If you want to awaken your luck, I believe these are the rules you must follow. Give them a try. They say that those who don't believe in luck have never experienced success. In conclusion, luck is inherently present in everyone, but it lies dormant within us. If we don't awaken that dormant luck, it will remain asleep within us for a lifetime. To become a lucky person, all we need to do is awaken the luck within ourselves. We need to ring the alarm bell to awaken the luck within us. Remember these 7 words. They will create our luck.

Visitor : So, do I just need to remember the 7 keywords?

Mentor: No, you shouldn't just remember the keywords alone. You need to follow specific practical methods of applying those keywords. Let me briefly introduce my own method as an example. Just take it as a reference. Whenever I face a challenging task, I try to apply these principles as much as possible. Surprisingly, the task progresses smoothly and easily.

Visitor: It would be great if you could provide more specific examples.

Mentor: OK. There is something that I have been fully immersed in recently. It's learning how to sew with a sewing machine. I am also applying this to '7 Keywords of Good Luck'. First, for number 1, Sherpa, I started with self-study, but I felt my limits. So I went to find a Sherpa who could help me in this field. It's a lifelong learning center operated by the city. I found a sewing machine instructor there to be my Sherpa. For number 2, surfer, I started with a small household sewing machine, but I thought I had to use an industrial sewing machine to do it properly someday, so I learned how to use an industrial sewing machine. For number 3, golfer, if I want to learn sewing skills, I have to learn in detail, from various reforms to repairs and clothing production. For number 4, escaping slavery, it's not enough to just participate in the learning center program chronically. To increase the effectiveness, I also upload the works I have made on YouTube by filming them every time.

Visitor : Are you even filming and uploading videos to YouTube?

Mentor: That's right. It's like killing two birds with one stone, learning sewing skills and uploading YouTube videos. To review what I've learned each week, I summarize the completed projects and record them in a notebook for future reference, like a chess or a baduk player. Learning at the lifelong learning center was difficult at first, especially since I was the only man, but I overcame it well and now I'm doing well. From the archery instructor, I learned the importance of starting, which is the beginning. I carefully considered my decision and started, and now I continue to improve my skills by learning one work after another. In the future, I will be able to repair my own clothes and even reform my wife's clothes, and I will be able to give my future grandchildren wonderful props or clothes. By thinking about this rule in everything I do, things seem to flow naturally and I feel lucky. This is how I create my own luck, one step at a time.

Visitor : Wow! It's amazing that a man is learning sewing, and even applying it to the 7 laws of awakening luck. I really understand it well. It seems like luck is something we create for ourselves. So, it's not that I don't have luck, but rather that I haven't awakened it yet.

Mentor: That's right. It's not about having or not having luck, but about awakening it or not. All you need to do is awaken your dormant luck. In other words, it is important to gradually make the characteristics of the 7 keywords your own. Remember that.

Visitor : That's really awesome. We can easily remember all seven characteristics of a person. I definitely want to put it into practice. By the way, when you were explaining about learning from the sixth athlete in the Triathlon and mentioned that the first condition for happiness is having a mature defense mechanism to overcome hardships, I could really empathize a lot. So, are there separate conditions for creating the happiness that we desire? Could you please explain that in more detail?

Mentor: It is not only a great topic for conversation but also essential content. What do you think is the reason why we should diligently prepare for retirement?

Visitor : Could it be that we strive to prepare for retirement in order to become happier in our old age?

Mentor: That's correct. It's to become happier in our old age. However, there are ways for us to anticipate the happiness in old age even before turning 60. It means that the happiness in old age can significantly vary depending on the conditions people have prepared in advance, even before reaching the age of 60.

Visitor : Are you saying that depending on the conditions people have prepared, they can have a glimpse of the level of happiness in old age even before turning 60?

Mentor: That is a very important point mentioned in the book I mentioned earlier, 'The Conditions of Happiness.' Let me briefly explain those conditions. I express them as the 7 conditions that determine the level of happiness in old age. In fact, these findings are based on extensive research conducted at Harvard University in the United States. Before discussing this aspect, let me first ask you a question. How do you think happiness is created? If there are conditions for achieving happiness, what do you think those conditions might be?

Visitor : Well, I suppose having some money, good health, and all family members doing well would be enough, wouldn't it?

Mentor: As we live, we experience moments of happiness, joy, and satisfaction that unexpectedly come to us. Someone once said that happiness is a journey, not a final destination. This probably means that happiness should be felt in every moment, rather than being determined by receiving a report card and judging happiness based on those grades. Isn't there a movie called 'Happiness Is Not in Grades,' right?

So, how can we attain such happiness? Can we simply obtain happiness without any preparation? How wonderful would that be? However, that's not the case. The important thing is that each individual's happiness in old age is largely determined by the conditions of happiness they have established before turning 60.

Visitor : It seems like you have a valid reason for saying that, don't you?

Mentor: That's correct. I'm not talking about myself, but rather sharing the results of a famous study.

Visitor : You said it's a famous study result?

Mentor: I'll briefly introduce it. Professor Alibek, a professor of medicine at Harvard University in the United States, started a longitudinal study called the 'Grant Study' on human life with 268 Harvard sophomores as subjects. During the study, he passed away, and another medical professor at Harvard, Professor George Vaillant, continued the study for a total of 72 years. After completing the study, Professor George Vaillant put the results in a book called 'The Conditions of Happiness'. The most important key point of the book is that the degree of happiness in old age can be determined by how 7 elements are prepared. That's why it's called the '7 Conditions of Happiness'.

Visitor : 72 years of research? That's a really long time for a study. But what does this research mean for retirees?

Mentor: Take a moment to think about it. Ultimately, as we prepare for the golden years of our lives after retirement, we do so with the aim of living a purposeful life that we pursue. If we could know the conditions for happiness in old age in advance, we would be able to prepare for it in a more concrete and systematic manner.

Visitor: The statement suggests knowing the conditions for happiness in old age in advance and preparing for it accordingly. Well, first of all, we should find out what are the seven conditions for happiness. What are they?

Seven conditions of happiness

Mentor: That's right. You understand it well. If we know the conditions for happiness in advance, prepare well for our '4 areas of retirement preparation', and create our 'Self-core brand', then the quality of happiness in old age can be higher. After hearing all seven conditions, you can understand how important the 4 areas of retirement preparation we are trying to prepare for right now are.

Visitor : It seems that the seven conditions for happiness, the 4 areas of retirement preparation, and the concept of Self-core brand can all be interconnected. I'm even more fascinated by the seven conditions for happiness.

Mentor: Alright. So, from now on, I'll briefly convey the seven conditions for happiness. Among these seven conditions, the first condition that predicts the level of happiness in our old age is called 'Mature defense mechanisms'. Although it may sound a bit complicated, in simple terms, it refers to the attitude of how well we can overcome hardships when they come. Essentially, if we don't handle these difficulties well and fail to overcome them, we can fall into great unhappiness and never achieve true happiness. It means that we need to become strong in the face of crises. Even if we live well in our daily lives, unexpected hardships and crises can happen to anyone, and if we cannot overcome them, happiness will become distant. To achieve this, the research recommends cultivating patience, adopting a positive mindset, and equipping ourselves with humor.

7 conditions of Happiness

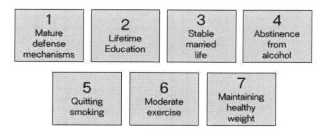

| 1 Mature defense mechanisms | 2 Lifetime Education | 3 Stable married life | 4 Abstinence from alcohol |
| 5 Quitting smoking | 6 Moderate exercise | 7 Maintaining healthy weight | |

Visitor : I completely empathize. It seems to be correct. Behind the success stories of successful people, there are always stories of those who overcame difficulties. I now have a unique determination to overcome difficulties well when they come my way.

Mentor: Good!. Then, in order to overcome these difficulties and hardships after retirement, what should we do? The research suggests that we should cultivate patience, have a positive attitude towards life, and be armed with humor, among other things. Do you think that's enough? Don't you think the solution is too vague? Therefore, my argument is that if you have prepared enough for the 4 areas of retirement preparation, Sollive, Comlive, Challive, and Vollive, and continue to develop your solitude empowerment, you can easily overcome the difficulties that come your way. More specifically, you can prevent such difficulties from arising in the first place to a large extent. Do you understand what I mean?

Visitor : Ah, I see. If one takes responsibility for their own future life and prepares for it step by step, it seems that many difficulties and hardships will disappear, and even if they arise, they will have the inner strength to overcome them. So, what is the second thing then?

Mentor: The second condition for happiness that can predict the degree of happiness in our old age is lifetime education.

The attitude of continuously learning and challenging oneself even as one ages becomes a very important factor for happiness in old age.

Visitor : How unexpected! So the second one is lifetime education. It's interesting that having a mindset of always learning becomes an important factor for happiness.

Mentor: Take a look at this as well. Aren't we doing Challive? Isn't Challive essentially lifetime education?

Visitor : I see. Then what is the third one?

Mentor: The third condition for happiness is a stable married life. It's such an obvious statement, isn't it? A stable married life is truly an essential factor that takes responsibility for our happiness in old age. According to research findings, losing one's family has a greater impact on unhappiness than losing one's health. To maintain a harmonious and stable married life, the efforts of both spouses are necessary. Particularly, the role of the retired husband is emphasized to some extent.

Visitor: This also aligns with the saying that service starts from home, the first condition of Vollive. I feel the importance of the 4 areas of retirement preparation.

Mentor: Let me once again specifically address the actions that couples should take for a stable married life, especially regarding the role of the husband.

Visitor: Understood. It appears that the role of the husband is indeed crucial. Please continue to elaborate on the conditions for happiness.

Mentor: The fourth condition for predicting the level of happiness in old age is abstaining from excessive drinking. Even if you do drink, it is advised to do so in moderation. As we age, alcohol can become a culprit that takes away various aspects of our happiness. Research has shown that alcohol can adversely affect our health, finances, and even our reputation and dignity, making moderation in drinking an essential factor for happiness in old age. While it is often said to enjoy in moderation, it is not as easy as it sounds.

Visitor : Sure. What is the fifth one then?

Mentor: The fifth condition for predicting the level of happiness in old age is quitting smoking. Smoking is truly detrimental for various reasons. Moving on, the sixth one is exercise. It may not require any further explanation, but if we were to mention one habit that should never be discarded even in old age, it would be exercise. I believe we can all easily agree on that.

Visitor : I often think that exercise becomes even more necessary as we age. So, one more is left. What is it?

Mentor: The seventh and final condition for determining the level of happiness in old age is maintaining a healthy weight. It is considered a crucial factor in the happiness of old age to be able to maintain a healthy weight through exercise, as well as dietary habits and lifestyle choices. So, we have looked at these seven factors. Of course, there are many other factors that contribute to happiness, but these results are drawn from research conducted by experts on human lifespan, which is the longest-running study in the world. However, the important thing here is that individuals who have already achieved five to six or more of these seven factors in their 50s, before turning 60, are almost always happy and healthy by the time they reach 80. On the other hand, the study revealed that individuals with three or fewer factors had no one who was happy or healthy.

Visitor: According to the findings of the study, individuals who have three or fewer out of the seven happiness factors mentioned are not happy at all. I am also not currently in a satisfying state, so I should start making changes from now on.

Mentor: Good! That's exactly the point. In order for someone to become happy, they need to create certain conditions, and the question is: what is the method for creating those conditions? Simply making a resolution is not enough, is it? It's important to have something to start with and how to start. Most people stop at just having the intention. It should be followed by action, shouldn't it? Didn't they say, "Thinking is not doing"? Perhaps there should be specific tools to translate it into action. That's precisely the essence of what I'm talking about: using the tools of the '4 Areas of Retirement Preparation' and 'Self-core brand' to create your own core brand.

Visitor : I see. Now I understand why this model is important. I understood exactly what the 7 conditions for predicting happiness in old age are. Now, I need to create happiness on my own through specific preparations in the '4 Areas of Retirement Preparation'. There are so many feelings that I am experiencing today.

Mentor: Your attitude towards learning is exemplary. You have so many qualities that make for a good retiree.

Visitor : Thank you for your kind words. However, you mentioned earlier that the roles between spouses are important for a stable married life, especially the role of the retired husband. Even though I want to be good to my wife after retirement, it's not working out well. What can I do? While my relationship with my wife hasn't been necessarily bad up until now, given my previous emphasis on my career, it now feels difficult for me to prioritize her. I'm a bit worried about how to be better for her after retirement.

Mentor: Most husbands have common issues, it's a given. There are always unexpected issues that you never thought of before retirement. I've also experienced this problem to a great extent. Shall I share the secret with you?

Visitor : Is it true that you have a secret?

Mentor: Yes, I do. The secret is to turn your wife into a debtor.

Turn Your wife into a Debtor

Visitor : Did you tell me to turn my wife into a debtor? What do you mean?

Mentor: Do you have gratitude towards your wife who has supported you to be successful in your career?

Visitor : Yes, I am very grateful.

Mentor: I understand that sentiment very well. I felt the same way. When I was about to retire, I truly felt grateful to my wife. After successfully completing 35 years of work, I entered a relatively happy retirement life, and I deeply appreciated my wife's support throughout all those years. We may not be wealthy, but we have an apartment and a small building that generates monthly rental income. Our children have also grown up well, each fulfilling their own roles. Whenever we faced big or small difficulties, my wife handled them wisely and supported me. I am incredibly thankful to her. It feels like I owe her a great debt. I had a momentary thought that I am indebted to my wife. So, from now on, I want to gradually repay the debt to my wife. I want to settle all debts and eventually make my wife feel like she owes me, transforming her into my debtor. That is my goal.

Visitor : Oh, that's a remarkable statement. It suggests repaying the debt to our wife and even treating her in a way that makes her feel indebted. So, how do you plan to repay that debt?

Mentor: I express it as 'Three secrets to making your wife a debtor'. Give it a listen and if you can relate, try following my secrets. It may feel a bit awkward at first, but as you keep doing it, you'll gradually get the hang of it and it won't feel difficult. I'm still not perfect, but I'm improving a lot. My wife also really likes it.

Visitor : Three secrets to making your wife a debtor? I'm really curious. Please tell me quickly!

Mentor: Alright! Here we go. The first of the three secrets to making your wife a debtor is to use the 'Bravo Flattery Technique' on your wife.

3 secretes to making your wife a debtor

Bravo Flattery Technique	Ding Dong Dang Listening Technique	Vitamin Love Technique

Visitor : Bravo Flattery technique? What exactly is that?

Mentor: Yes, it's called the Bravo flattery technique. Although I can't recall the exact name, a prominent American female novelist once advised against getting married before learning the flattery technique. She particularly emphasized that flattery from a husband is the ultimate weapon of communication between spouses and a shortcut. The British playwright Bernard Shaw stated, "No one has ever been sued or had to pay money for flattery in history." In my words, flattery is a specific behavior that turns the other person into a respected and valuable individual, a strategic technique of compliments that brings mutual happiness and embodies the highest form of altruism. In simple terms, flattery towards a wife by a husband can become the basic value of repaying even a small portion of the past debts. For example, saying things like 'Because of you, I was able to successfully navigate my career. I am sincerely grateful,' or 'The soybean paste stew you cooked tastes even better than any other in this world!' These are the specific forms of flattery that can be used in various situations. You will notice a change in the atmosphere at home after a day or two. However, flattery is not always easy. Even if you try to flatter, it may not be readily accepted from the beginning. That's why when it comes to flattery, you should use not just any flattery, but 'Bravo flattery'.

Visitor : Bravo flattery?

Mentor: Bravo is the enthusiastic applause and praise that the audience throws when a person on stage performs well in a concert or musical performance. If the person on stage does not sing or play with sincerity, they cannot expect such heartfelt applause from the audience. Similarly, in the context of flattery, it means sincerely flattering someone to receive applause from them. Even if you do this well, you can avoid conflicts, but it's not easy. At first, people who don't usually do it may wonder why they should do it. They may have various misunderstandings or feel uncomfortable, but keep trying. The atmosphere in the household will truly change. Apply the techniques of Bravo flattery to your wife.

Visitor : I see. The technique of Bravo flattery truly seems like a great strategy. It appears that flattery is often the most vulnerable area for husbands. I should start implementing it right away as well. So, what is the second secret?

Mentor: The second secret of 'Three secrets to making your wife a debtor' is to utilize the skill of "Ding Dong Dang Active Listening," which means listening attentively to every word your wife says. Communication between spouses ultimately revolves around exchanging messages, and the fundamental reason for failed message delivery is often the poor quality of the relationship. Therefore, in order to have effective communication between spouses, it is necessary to first improve the quality of the relationship. The first step in improving the relationship is to listen carefully to your partner's words. However, most husbands struggle with this. They simply don't know how to listen until the end. The important thing here is not just to listen but to practice 'Ding Dong Dang Active Listening'. Ding Dong Dang Active Listening is not too difficult. First, husbands should listen attentively, allowing their wives to finish their stories. This is the 'Ding' part. The 'Dong' part involves affirming and positively responding to your wife's words by saying "Yeah! Yeah! You're right! You're right!" and nodding your head. Lastly, the 'Dang' part is a crucial tip. It involves throwing in well-timed, good questions that your wife wants to hear. This is the essence of Ding Dong Dang Active Listening.

Visitor : It's really fun. But why is it called Ding Dong Dang Active Listening?

Mentor: What does Ding Dong Dang mean? It means passing the test, specifically the passing point of active listening. It requires going through these three stages to pass. By doing so, the wife will truly feel that her husband is not on the other side, but on her side. Just by doing this, the wife's feelings of resentment and injustice will melt away like snow. By doing just this, a significant portion of the debt to the wife is repaid. Fully listening to the wife's words until the end, 'Ding Dong Dang Active Listening' is the second secret.

Visitor: Listening to my wife's words attentively, providing appropriate responses, and even asking positive questions she wants to hear, that's the second secret of 'Ding Dong Dang Active Listening.' I used to think that making my wife happy meant only buying material things like luxury bags, but it seems that's not the case. It's about impressing my wife through good actions. While it's nice that it doesn't require spending money, I'm not sure if I can do it well. So, what is the third secret then?

Mentor: One thing is certain, everyone finds it difficult at first, but with practice, they can do it well. Quoting the words of Immanuel Kant, a German poet and philosopher, which I often use, it's applicable in moments like this. 'Everything was difficult before it became easy', isn't that a great quote? Ultimately, it's a matter of doing or not doing, rather than being good or bad at it. Now, let me introduce the final secret to making your wife a debtor. The third secret among the three secrets is to apply love skills like vitamins to your wife.

Visitor : You mean love skills like vitamins? It's not just love skills, but love skills that are like vitamins? Does that mean it's a healthy love skill? I'm really curious again!

Mentor: Let me explain. There is a very popular British novelist among many people. His name is Alain de Botton. This novelist said, 'Love is not passion, but a skill'. According to him, we may have a good understanding of how love begins, but we are not very knowledgeable about how love is sustained. That's because love starts with emotions, which everyone can easily feel, but sustaining love is a skill that we are not well-informed about. Therefore, love is a skill that cannot be acquired without learning. Ultimately, maintaining a harmonious married life without ever properly learning the skill of love can be very reckless and risky. The American psychoanalyst Erich Fromm also said, 'Love is not a problem of spontaneous emotion, but a practice and a learned skill'. So, what do you think is the best and most promising skill of love that we should learn?

Visitor : The skill of love, the most promising one? Well, I'm not sure!

Mentor: Alain de Botton said that the most promising skill of love in this world is knowing how to make the other person laugh. Wow! That's exactly it. Do you not fully understand with that statement? If a husband knows how to make his wife laugh and puts it into action, wouldn't it skyrocket her satisfaction with her husband? Laughter is probably the best vitamin for a wife. Making your wife laugh every day is like offering her a daily dose of vitamin. If the days are filled with laughter like this, it feels like the husband has finally repaid his debts to his wife, and from now on, the wife may feel like she owes the husband a little bit instead. Is this just my own thought? What do you think?

Visitor : Wow, I'm really impressed too! You mentioned that the most promising skill of love in this world is knowing how to make the other person smile. That's such a wonderful statement. Making your wife smile is indeed crucial. That's why you referred to it as the 'vitamin-like skill of love'. Ultimately, it means doing things that can make the other person happy. I can relate to that. When I watch movies, I often see older foreign couples holding hands and walking in the park, smiling and looking so happy. It makes me think that when I grow old, I want to age beautifully like that. But to achieve that, continuous effort is necessary. It's truly an inspiring lecture. Could you please summarize the 3 secrets to turning my wife into a debtor once again?

Mentor: I'm glad to hear that you were listening well. So, once again, let me summarize the 3 secrets to turning your wife into a debtor. First, challenge your wife with the 'Bravo Flattery Technique'. Second, learn the skill of active listening by truly listening to your wife until the end with the 'Ding Dong Dang Listening Technique'. And finally, the third secret is to understand how to make your wife smile, which is the ultimate skill of love, and make efforts to put it into action with the 'Vitamin Love Technique'. Of course, it won't be easy to fully repay the debts to my wife accumulated over time. However, it's important to strive to repay any debts to your wife until the end of your life. While turning your wife into a debtor may not be realistically achievable, it symbolizes the effort and dedication we put into our relationships.

Visitor : Initially, when you mentioned turning your wife into a debtor, I was intrigued about what you meant. But now it's clear. Your lecture, expressed paradoxically, has left a deep impression. However, have you fully repaid your debts to your wife? Have you turned your wife into a debtor?

Mentor: I'm still in the process of repaying. It seems like I haven't even paid back 50% yet. I'm still working hard to pay off the debts. I am doing my best in my own way to practice Bravo Flattery, but the response doesn't seem to be very positive so far. However, I can feel that things are gradually improving. There have been requests for making small flower pots and altering skirts to me. Every morning when I leave for the office, my wife even sees me off at the front door. These are clear signs of a changed atmosphere. During conversations, I make sure to listen attentively and provide plenty of support, following the Ding Dong Dang method. I keeps asking my wife good questions, which leads to longer and more diverse conversations. I also try to do cute actions that can bring laughter and be the best vitamin for my wife, although I'm not very good at it. I've been consistently making 500 dishes for my wife until I die. I even wrote lyrics and produced an album for her, titled 'My Wife Within Me.' And for my wife's 60th birthday, I'm practicing shoulder keyboard and drums every day to hold a small concert. Recently, I compiled the writings I've written about my wife into a book and gave it to her as a gift. The title of the poetry collection is 'Life Shorts (My Wife Edition)'.

Visitor : You truly are a practitioner who puts all these teachings into action. That's remarkable. However, I assume you also know well, having worked for many years, that in my case, as I approach retirement, my relationship with my wife isn't necessarily bad, but it feels a bit lackluster. I would like to turn this situation around in a more progressive direction. Do you have any advice or words of wisdom to share?

Mentor: I felt that the relationship between my wife and I had become quite lackluster around the time of my retirement. As I had more time to spend with my wife after retiring, I gradually realized that our relationship had become somewhat neglected. Let me suggest a solution for that. This is a method that I have personally used and continue to use to this day.

Visitor : You have also experienced such cases. What is the secret to resolving it?

Mentor: This is not a secret, just something that seems so obvious that we might miss it. Anyway, I have found that following this principle not only improves my relationship with my wife but also creates a fresh and positive atmosphere.

Visitor : I was quite hesitant about whether to ask this question or not, but it seems like I made a good decision.

Mentor: Before I explain the solution, let me first explain the background as to why a once happy couple may become distant at the time of retirement. When someone finishes a long career and enters retirement, naturally, they spend more time with their spouse. However, these moments can feel somewhat awkward, and it becomes uncertain how to spend that time together. I believe there are quite a few individuals who can relate to this situation, even though they may not openly express it. According to a survey, approximately 45% of wives of retirees responded that their retired husbands became bothersome. Furthermore, the average amount of time couples spend together, excluding sleeping hours, is 4 hours and 10 minutes, and there were even responses indicating a desire to reduce that time. Additionally, another survey revealed that the most impossible thing in this world is to have respect for a retired husband, ranking it as the top answer. Although it is a somewhat lighthearted survey result.

Visitor : Wow, that's quite a lighthearted survey result. Still, how come they consider it the most impossible thing? I guess it just goes to show how challenging it is.

Mentor: Yes, that's right. In this situation, where should a retired husband go now? Many retired husbands may feel frustrated, but what can we do? Frustration is one thing, but we can't seem to find a solution. So, is there really no way to revitalize a relationship that has become lax like this? In order to revive a relationship that has become lax, I believe we need to rebuild the foundation from the ground up. Only then can the relationship between the couple be fundamentally restored. That's the method I want to share with you today.

Visitor : So, it seems we need to rebuild from the ground up. Then, what are the specific ways to build a solid foundation?

Rebuild marital foundation

Mentor: Rebuilding a deteriorated marital relationship from the ground up involves two main aspects. The first is accepting one's spouse as they are, which may come as an unexpected answer. However, it is truly crucial. Accepting one's spouse as they are means respecting them for who they are at present. It is known as the most challenging task among married middle-aged couples. When the renowned French scholar Dominique Wolton, known as the founder of communication, came to Korea to give a lecture, someone asked him about the essence of communication between married couples. In response, Wolton stated that accepting one's spouse as they are is the first signal of respect. Accepting one's spouse as they are seems to be incredibly vital. It is like performing CPR for communication in a marital relationship, where you let go of a little bit of yourself and accept a bit more of your spouse.

Visitor : Like performing CPR, which opens up the airways and saves lives, right?

2 ways to rebuild marital foundation

Accept one's spouse as they are	Avoid Unnecessary argument

Mentor: Absolutely. I am also active as a safety instructor with five first-class safety certifications. Among them, CPR is incredibly important. Do you know how long the golden time for CPR is? It's only four minutes. Within those four minutes, a matter of life and death is at stake. However, there is also a golden time for communication between couples, just like CPR. If you miss the golden time for communication between spouses, it cannot be restored. In the context of a marital relationship, such communication must be firmly established as the foundation for the coexistence of the couple to be practically possible. When asked about the secret to the best marital alchemy by Mr. John Beta, the husband of the longest-living couple in the U.S. at the age of 104, he reportedly answered as follows: "It is accepting your spouse as they are. The very idea of trying to change your spouse is madness." I myself have not been able to fulfill this aspect well throughout my life. Now, trying to put this into practice, I realize it's not as easy as it sounds. It seems that the foundation was not firmly established. That's why I am currently making efforts to reinforce the foundation work as much as possible. How about you? Do you have a solid foundation?

Visitor: No, I haven't fully accepted my wife as she is either. It seems like a really important point, isn't it? I'll make an effort. Thank you for your kind words. Each and every word you've said today remains in my heart. Now, what is another thing I should work on, like the foundation construction?

Mentor: The second aspect of the foundational work to rebuild the deteriorated relationship between the couple is to always avoid unnecessary arguments with your spouse. Many of us have experienced that conflicts between couples often start from trivial arguments. Insisting only on one's own logic without any compromise can be the cause of disputes. It is truly foolish to solely pursue winning over your spouse without any concessions. We have often realized that most arguments between couples are insignificant in the long run, haven't we? Let's think back to our younger days. There is a famous British singer named Calvin Harris. Among the songs he sings, there is a song called 'Sweet Nothing'.

Visitor : Are you referring to Calvin Harris' song 'Sweet Nothing'? I also enjoy that song!

Mentor: Wow! You know that song. In the lyrics, there is a part that goes 'I'm living on such sweet nothing.' It is supposed to convey the meaning of a sweet and precious thing. During the early days of a romantic relationship, lovers exchange many sweet but meaningless words and create a blooming love. Isn't that a time when everything feels sweet without any fights? You also have those experiences. I'm a bit embarrassed to say this, but I have those experiences as well. I remember laughing so much with my newlywed wife that we laughed all night long whenever we mentioned the word 'jin'. We laughed for more than an hour after saying 'jin ramen' (a type of Korean instant noodle). It was like we laughed all the happy laughs we could in our lives. We were completely crazy. But looking back, I think those were the happiest moments. However, I realized that these Sweet Nothings are not worthless in life and have some significant meaning. But after marriage, these words can become meaningless and useless, and couples can argue about small and meaningless things. This can escalate into bigger arguments and eventually start a war between them.

Visitor : That's right. I also have those kinds of situations often.

Mentor: The important thing to keep in mind here is that what our spouse says is never a useless talk. Even seemingly insignificant words have their own meaning. It means that we should accept each other's opinions as Sweet Nothings, not as Nothing. It's like a word that made us laugh for an hour with just one word, like 'Jin Ramyeon'. Experts say that through these seemingly useless conversations, couples communicate with each other and experience fun. I believe this is a crucial key to avoiding arguments and eliminating conflicts between spouses.

Visitor : Ah, I see. Now I understand why the relationship between couples has become strained. I can strongly relate to your suggestion of starting from the basics and rebuilding the foundation. You have provided two methods for repairing the strained relationship from the ground up. The first is accepting your spouse as they are, and the second is to always avoid unnecessary arguments and enjoy Sweet Nothings together. It seems like each of my life's assignments is being resolved one by one. You truly carry so much wisdom within you. It's impressive how you have the ability to put everything into practice and make it your own. I wonder where that strength comes from.

Mentor: I am not sure how to respond to your excessive praise. If I were to say, I believe that power probably comes from my diligent note-taking habit. I used to have a habit of taking notes, and after retiring, I'm making even more effort to diligently take notes. Being a good note-taker is essential for survival. As I get older, I tend to forget things more often, so I write things down without fail. I have notepads in seven different places around me. From jotting down daily tasks to keeping monthly schedules, it's a basic practice. I keep them on my desk, in the car, by the bed, in the shower, and even inside my clothes, so I can write down ideas whenever they come to me. It's truly important.

Visitor : So, what do you usually take notes on?

Mentor: I record everything starting from my schedule. Especially good ideas should be recorded immediately so as not to forget. I even jot down useful information for lectures, interesting and funny stories. I write them all down using notepads, my phone, notebooks, calendars, and more.

When these accumulate every day, they become a great treasure.

Visitor : Ah, I see. I think it's a habit that I should definitely develop as well. However, I have another concern. I feel like I'm someone who speaks very boringly, even in my own opinion. Even when I try to be funny or say something interesting, it just doesn't seem to work. Do you happen to have any useful tips for people who speak boringly?

Mentor: Most middle-aged men are like that. They've lived in that kind of social atmosphere until now, so it's not easy to change. Another person who visited me a while ago had a similar concern. He was retired. He naturally had more time to talk with his family and have personal conversations by going to personal gatherings after retiring. However, no one seems to be very interested in what he says. Even his wife is not very interested in talking to him, and even the children do not want to have long conversations if they feel the generation gap. He is not very comfortable even when he goes out to gatherings. In fact, he doesn't have much to say, so he mainly listens to other people's stories, and even if he has a chance to speak, he is confused about what to say and often comes back without saying anything.

Visitor : That's right. I'm exactly in that situation now. Is there any solution for that?

Mentor: Yes, there is. In short, to become a popular person anywhere, even for those who are truly uninteresting, it seems that they need something new as a weapon when speaking. I would like to introduce three secret conversation techniques that I am using in various ways. These methods can be considered as truly useful conversation secrets for couples who find their conversations dull, for those who feel disconnected from the younger generation in conversations, and for those who become completely overlooked at gatherings.

Visitor : Is there really such a secret technique? I'm eager to hear about it quickly.

3 tips to turn boring people into aces

Mentor: Among the three useful conversation techniques for boring speakers, the first one is to memorize always-applicable nonsense quizzes.

Visitor : Nonsense quizzes, you say?

Mentor: Yes, nonsense quizzes. The usage of these quizzes is really broad. They can be frequently used in everyday conversations, greetings at meetings with occasional opportunities, and even for people like me who give lectures. Just a few of them can make people burst out laughing. By utilizing a few nonsense quizzes, you can easily receive compliments like "You're really fun!".

3 tips to turn boring people into aces

Memorize Nonsense Quizzes	Learn Trend Slang	Polish Light Dad jokes

Visitor : For example, what are some of them?

Mentor: Let me give you an example. Here's one of the nonsense quizzes that I often use in face-to-face lectures, starting with 'In this world'. Alright, here's the question. In this world, what is the favorite food of the iron?

Visitor : The favorite food of the iron in this world? I'm not sure.

Mentor: The answer is pizza. It means that you need to pronounce 'pizza' well in Korean. Nonsense quizzes often involve homonyms in the language of that country. Here, the Korean pronunciation of pizza has the meaning of flattening well-crumpled clothes.

Visitor: Ah, I see! Indeed, anyone who knows Korean would understand it. That sounds really fun! I should use it right away today.

Mentor: You should prepare topics to talk about in advance through nonsense quizzes like this, and keep using them. Even if the initial reaction around you doesn't seem good, it can be really fun if you keep doing it. Try to jot down interesting things in your everyday life and make use of them. It will make you a very interesting person.

Visitor: That seems like a pretty good approach. I already feel a bit more confident. So, what is the second secret then?

Mentor: The second of the three conversation tips for people who talk boringly is to learn trendy slang among young people. It can have a great effect when talking to young people.

Visitor : Learning trendy slang?

Mentor: That's right! It's something that you should definitely learn as you get older. The biggest difference in generational gaps felt by young people from older people is not in behavior, thinking, or possessions, but rather in language used in conversations. Slang, in particular, is the most obvious characteristic of this. If we learn a few trendy slang words and use them occasionally, we might have a good opportunity to narrow the gap with the younger generation, including our children.

Visitor: Learning trendy slang, huh? I really don't know the words that kids these days use. Could you give me an example?

Mentor: Trendy slang words are mostly abbreviations. They are created by combining the initial letters of each word to form a compound word that is used as a single word. This will be easily understood by Korean speakers. Now, let me give you a question. It's the easiest word among the trendy slang words. What does the word 'wan-nae-seu' mean in Korean trendy slang?

Visitor : I'm not sure what 'wan-nae-seu' means.

Mentor: You don't know the answer. So, young people feel like they have difficulty communicating with older people. When young people see these words, they are very natural words. So, we don't need to know all the slang words, but if we intentionally learn a few and use them in conversations occasionally, young kids will really like it. This can also be a starting point for children to feel that they can communicate well with parents.

Visitor : I really need to learn it. It seems very useful. By the way, what was the answer to that question?

Mentor: I see, 'wan-nae-seu' is it? 'Wan-nae-seu' is a term used in Korean, which is a shortened form of 'wanjeon nae style' and it means something is completely one's own preferred style. It's a trendy slang term that young people in Korea are very familiar with.

Visitor: That sounds really interesting. Although it feels like our Korean language is being affected, it seems necessary to learn a little for better communication with young people. This is definitely a good tip as well. So, what is the third tip then?

Mentor: Among the three useful conversation tips for people who speak boringly, the third golden tip is to polish your repertoire of light dad jokes that can bring laughter to people. Even just incorporating slang and nonsense quizzes can greatly enhance the fun in conversations with others, but having one or two light dad jokes can consistently bring joy to the people around you. However, it's even better if those dad jokes contain a positive message.

Visitorr : A dad joke with a message? Can you also introduce just one of those?

Mentor: Sure! Let me share a very interesting food delivery story with you. Alright, here we go. There was a Chinese restaurant called 'Bullet Chinese Restaurant.' They were known for their incredibly fast delivery service, so I would often order food from them. One day, my wife didn't feel like cooking, so I ordered two plates of Jajangmyeon (black bean noodles). They delivered it to me in a flash, just like a bullet. As I was enjoying the delicious Jajangmyeon, I found a chess piece inside. I was so angry that I called the Chinese restaurant and said, "What's going on? There's a chess piece in my Jajangmyeon." The owner replied, "Congratulations! You've won the Tangsuyuk (sweet and sour pork) prize. We'll send you a plate of Tangsuyuk within 20 minutes." And guess what? The Tangsuyuk actually arrived. Isn't that a clever comeback?

Visitor : Ha! Ha! That's a really funny dad joke. I think anyone would find this story amusing, don't you think?

Mentor: That's right. Anyone would find this story amusing. The point is to deliver a message through such an entertaining story. My intention is to convey the message that everyone should learn how to stay calm and handle difficult situations well, just like the Chinese restaurant owner, no matter what challenging circumstances they may face.

Visitor: I see. It's really interesting and informative. If I were to summarize the three useful conversation tips for people who speak in a boring way, as you presented earlier, the first would be to memorize nonsense quizzes that can always be used. The second would be to learn trendy slang among young people, and the third would be to practice witty dad jokes that can make people laugh. I got it. Thank you.

Mentor: In fact, these three methods are very helpful in leading interesting conversations with people of all ages and genders. However, it may not be easy for everyone to speak like this from the beginning, depending on their personality. But the important thing is to never give up and use them whenever there is an opportunity. Eventually, when you have conversations with other people or go out to gatherings, you will soon hear the reaction, "Do you have any other interesting stories today?".

Visitor : There is no doubt that these are really good tips. It gives me the confidence that I can become a really interesting person just by doing this. Thank you once again. I will work hard to prepare and try to use them often.

Mentor: That's right. It becomes easier as you keep trying. There is a saying that I always remind myself of whenever I try something new. I might have mentioned it a few times before. It's a quote from Johann Wolfgang von Goethe, a German philosopher and poet.

Visitor: I think I know that one. It's the saying, 'Everything was difficult before it became easy.' It's such a wonderful quote, I've also made sure to remember it.

Mentor: You're really like a sponge. You have a very quick learning ability. That's right. Just like Goethe's words, when you work hard, there comes a moment when things become easier. Do you know the joy of that moment? It's truly amazing. Well then, let's stop the morning lecture now. Let's have lunch and continue later, shall we?

Visitor : It's really a pleasant sound to hear while listening.

Mentor: I will personally make Jajangmyeon, black bean sauce noodles, for lunch. I have roughly prepared the ingredients, so it should take about 20 minutes to prepare.

Visitor: You seem to be good at both Western and Chinese cuisine. I never even dreamed that you could make Jajangmyeon yourself.

Mentor: It's simpler than you think. Shall we make it together?

He brought the ingredients from the refrigerator and neatly placed them on the dining table before starting his work. First, he coated a large wok with cooking oil and scooped the prepared black bean sauce into it, then he stir-fried it and transferred it into a separate dish. He mentioned that he buys pre-fried chunjang, but always gives it an extra stir-fry when making it. He explained that frying it slightly in oil is important to bring out the flavor of the Jajangmyeon. Next, he added pork and mirin to the wok and stir-fried them until cooked. Then, he added sugar, oyster sauce, soy sauce, and chicken stock to the wok, followed by potatoes, sweet potatoes, onions, cabbage, scallions, and other prepared vegetables. He stir-fried everything for a while and then added the previously stir-fried black bean sauce to the wok, mixing it together and letting it simmer. Finally, he adjusted the sauce thickness by adding a mixture of starch and water in a 1:2 ratio. Meanwhile, he boiled water in a separate pot to cook the noodles, mentioning that he uses special Chinese-style noodles. He emphasized that adding sweet potatoes gives the traditional Jajangmyeon its sweet flavor. The delicious aroma of Jajangmyeon stimulated the senses. In less than 20 minutes, two bowls of Jajangmyeon were ready. The two of them enjoyed their bowls, imitating each other's noodle-slurping like they were competing in a food challenge.

9

Growing Happiness with Age

Visitor : I really enjoyed the Jajangmyeon. Thank you so much. So, what class do we have in the afternoon?

Mentor: I have plenty of prepared topics, but it might be better to answer any specific questions you have rather than going through them. Is there anything you're curious about or would like to know as you're approaching retirement?

Visitor: I have so many things I'm interested in, I don't know where to start with my questions. Lately, as retirement day approaches, I sometimes feel that the status of husbands around me keeps diminishing. Especially as retirement approaches, it seems like I'm being ignored by my wife and family at home, and I constantly feel a sense of weakened competitiveness compared to other husbands. Is there any prescription for this?

Mentor: It's a sad story, but it's a realistic one that we face. It's also a common concern for many retirees. Every retiree goes through similar concerns. After retirement, retirees naturally have more time at home and more time to spend with their wives. However, over time, retirees start to feel like they are being treated like a child by their wives. In her book 'Keronroku', the famous Japanese writer, Sonoko Ayako, describe that husbands see their wives as furniture when they look at them. This is because, just like a table or a bed, you don't realize how important it is until it's gone. However, when wives look at their retired husbands, it's completely different. Do you know how they look at them?

Visitor : Well......

Mentor: According to the book, when a wife looks at her husband, she sees him as nothing more than a windbreaker for a hiking burner. She may find him necessary when the wind blows, but when the wind calms down, he becomes quite a cumbersome existence. As a result, the husband gradually loses his presence even within the household. On the other hand, as wives age, they tend to lead more active lives outside and receive compliments from others, while husbands often retain the tendency to criticize and educate their wives' behavior. This may be due to a sense of responsibility towards their wives, but it gradually causes husbands to lose their relative competitiveness. Therefore, emergency measures are needed to increase husbands' competitiveness regarding their wives. Wouldn't it be necessary to confidently regain the top position in terms of competitiveness towards one's wife?

Visitor : Of course, we need to regain the top spot. Do you have any special strategies or tricks up your sleeve? If you have any, please teach me.

Enhance husband's competitiveness

Mentor: I naturally have it. Let me introduce a very easy secret to you. First, remember these three words: military trainee, deer, broadcast anchor. If you only know these words, it should be enough to restore competitiveness among husbands. Husband's competitiveness will be regained, allowing our husband to reclaim the top spot in competitiveness.

3 hints to enhance husband's competitiveness

Visitor : The words 'military trainee, deer, broadcast anchor' as an emergency measure for restoring competitiveness for one's husband sounds interesting. What could be the meaning behind it?

Mentor: I will now explain the first emergency measure to restore competitiveness for one's husband. Among the three emergency measures to enhance competitiveness, the first one is to respond immediately when the wife calls, just like a military trainee.

Visitor : You mentioned that it's necessary to respond immediately when the wife calls, just like a military trainee. Is that the first method to improve the husband's competitiveness?

Mentor: Certainly. It means that when the wife calls, it is important to respond immediately, just like a military trainee. How are trainees trained? Don't they respond loudly and promptly when someone calls them? It is crucial for husbands to respond immediately when their wives call, as it is the first step in effective communication between spouses. According to marriage communication experts, husbands tend to be one beat behind when their wives call them. Every time this happens, the wife becomes displeased and angry. This small act of promptly responding is essential for smooth communication between spouses. It is said that there is an increasing number of husbands who ignore their wives' calls, ignore the prepared breakfast, and come late to eat, resulting in arguments and dissatisfaction. In any case, starting with the small practice of responding immediately when the wife calls, it becomes the foundation for improving the husband's competitiveness.

Visitor: So, your point is that the reason why the husband's competitiveness keeps decreasing is that there is poor communication between the couple, and the first step is to promptly respond when the wife calls. Otherwise, it causes discomfort to the wife and communication is disrupted from the beginning.

Mentor: Yes, that's right. Until now, because we were busy with work, we didn't have many opportunities to interact with my wife, so she was often displeased, but we just let it slide. However, after retirement, we started to have more frequent contact, and that's when my wife's dissatisfaction started to show outwardly. That's why we need to change this first. Even if you just practice this one thing well, your relationship with your wife will change a lot. I received a lot of compliments from my wife for just this one thing that changed after retirement.

Visitor : That's a very persuasive statement. I will definitely put it into practice as well. I will rejoin the military training center and become an excellent trainee. Now, what is the second word?

Mentor: The second emergency measure to improve a husband's competitiveness with his wife is to listen to her words like a deer.

Visitor : It seems like the advice is to listen to your wife's words attentively, just like a deer.

Mentor: That's correct. When a deer is eating, it stands its ears up and eats its food while still being aware of the outside world. It means that by listening, you can appropriately respond to the external world. Our husbands should do the same. By pricking up their ears and attentively listening to their wives, they can respond well. Listening to their wives' words raises their wives' presence and ultimately increases the husband's competitiveness. The American couples' counseling expert, Harville Hendrix, left the saying, "Happy wife, Happy life." It can be interpreted as the wife's happiness being the happiness of one's own life. What do you think?

Visitor : I completely agree. It's important to listen to your wife's words. Just by actively listening, the presence of the wife can increase. As a result, the husband's presence also increases, leading to enhanced competitiveness. Now, moving on to the third word, what is a 'broadcast anchor'.

Mentor: The third and final emergency measure to enhance a husband's competitiveness with regards to his wife is to speak about her strengths like a broadcast anchor. This can be considered the ultimate weapon for increasing a husband's competitiveness.

Visitor : The last method is to speak about your wife's strengths like a news anchor on TV. Did you say this is the ultimate weapon to increase a husband's competitiveness?

Mentor: Yes, that's right. Anchors on the news deliver a specific and clear explanation of a particular event to the viewers, don't they? Husbands are also encouraged to speak about their wives' strengths in such a specific manner, just like on the news. Moreover, husbands should seize every opportunity to express these strengths. Professor John Gottman, an American psychologist, talks about the '5:1 ratio' in conversations between couples that make relationships better. In other words, in order for a negative comment to be effectively conveyed between couples, there should be five preceding positive comments. By constantly discovering and praising their wives' strengths, husbands can deliver positive messages frequently, making it easier to convey negative messages in a gentle manner. By doing so, wives can feel the presence of their husbands. Naturally, the husband's competitiveness will increase. Do you agree?

Visitor: I completely agree. There are many reasons why a husband's competitiveness may decrease. If husbands follow this approach even after retirement, their wives will come to like them more and their competitiveness will also increase. These are really valuable words. Could you please summarize this point once again?

Mentor: To summarize again, there are three emergency measures to enhance a husband's competitiveness towards his wife. First, respond immediately when the wife calls, like a military trainee. Second, listen attentively to the wife's words, like a deer. Third, describe the wife's strengths in detail, like a broadcast anchor. If you remember these three words, military trainee, deer, and broadcast anchor, your husband's competitiveness will skyrocket. These three emergency measures are exactly what they sound like emergency measures. In other words, it means you should implement them quickly.

Visitor : I will start implementing the three points you mentioned from today in order to enhance my competitiveness and regain stability.

Mentor: I am also consistently putting this method into practice and heading towards stability. Let's meet at the peak.

Visitor : It seems like you have already reached the top, but I will do my best as you have taught me. I am learning so much today, step by step. If I continue like this, I won't be afraid of retiring. However, why do retirees keep fearing retirement? You mentioned some reasons why people fear retirement, but it would be helpful if you could summarize them all.

Mentor: I was actually planning to provide a summary. Before I discuss the four areas of retirement preparation, let me briefly mention the content I touched upon earlier. I will summarize it once again to ensure a clear understanding of the fundamental reasons why retirees fear retirement.

Visitor : I agree with you. So, what is the real reason why retirement is feared by everyone?

Are you afraid of retirement?

Mentor: First, let me share a bit about my own experience. Even though I made some retirement preparations when the retirement date approached, strangely enough, I started to feel a sense of fear. There wasn't any particular reason, but the fear kept growing, and I started losing sleep at night. I bought and read several retirement-related books, actively participated in retirement programs, consulted retirement experts, and sought advice from retired seniors. However, I couldn't find any specific guidelines on how to prepare for retirement, and the fear kept growing. In fact, according to a survey, 75% of people nearing retirement, including retired spouses, expressed fear of upcoming retirement. So, I conducted research. What is the real reason behind the fear of retirement? If we understand this, can't we better prepare for our old age? Upon investigation, I found that it could be represented by five reasons. Do you remember that I briefly mentioned these five reasons before?

Visitor : You mentioned it briefly. Since it seems to be an important part, could you please explain it in more detail?

Mentor: Certainly. I will explain each of the five reasons one by one.

Visitor : Thank you, sir.

Mentor: Let's find out the top 5 reasons why retirement is scary. I will explain them in reverse order, like a competition program. The 5th place is feeling like my worth is decreasing. In other words, I responded that my self-esteem seems to be crumbling. The term self-esteem was first used by American philosopher and psychologist 'William James'. He defined it as the mind that believes that one is a valuable person who is worthy of love and is capable of achieving some accomplishment. However, after retirement, this mindset rapidly declines.

5 reasons why retirement is scary

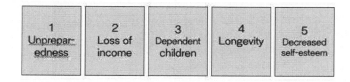

| 1 Unprepar- edness | 2 Loss of income | 3 Dependent children | 4 Longevity | 5 Decreased self-esteem |

Visitor : Your words suggest that self-esteem tends to significantly decline after retirement, and this can be one of the reasons why you may feel anxious about retiring. It appears quite possible. So, what is the 4th reason?

Mentor: The 4th reason among the top 5 real reasons why retirement is feared by everyone is that life after retirement feels too long. That's correct. As we are living in the era of centenarians, we are expected to live actively for more than 30 years after retirement. However, the prospect of having a long future ahead can evoke fear. According to the age classification proposed by the United Nations in 2015, youth starts at the age of 18 and lasts until 65, middle age starts at 66, and old age begins at 80. Even if one retires, they are still considered youth according to the UN's definition. It's natural to feel fearful about becoming a retiree when there is still a long way to go based on the suggested age classification.

Visitor : I'm also really afraid of this part. Retirement is coming soon, but I still feel like a young person. How can I be a retiree? I'm really worried about what to do after retirement in this kind of situation. So, what's the third content?

Mentor: Among the five real reasons why retirement is feared by everyone, the third one is having children to take care of. Taking care of children until the very end is considered a duty and role of parents, but until when should we be responsible for our children's future? And how far should we go in taking responsibility? It's a big homework for us. That's why it becomes a fear. I also have twin sons who are still unmarried, but it seems like my wife worries more than I do.

Visitor : I also worry a lot about my children. It seems like parents who are still in this generation would inevitably have the same anxiety and concerns. So, now that retirement is approaching, it makes these issues even more frightening. So, what is the second-ranked reason?

Mentor: The second-ranked reason among the five real reasons people fear retirement is that they no longer have a fixed source of income. As I who have been trying to prepare for retirement systematically, this is undoubtedly one of the biggest fears of retirement. However, experts say that after retirement, managing money is much more important than earning it, but many people still seem to be too focused only on making money. There is much to say about this issue, but I think that if you understand the points mentioned yesterday, you will be well prepared for financial matters.

Visitor: I Understood. So, what is the first reason people fear retirement? Although you mentioned it briefly yesterday, could you please elaborate on it a bit more?

Mentor: Okay. Of the five real reasons why people fear retirement, only one reason remains in the first place. However, this first place reason was chosen by far more people, a total of 65.1%, than the combined 2nd through 5th places. The top reason was that people responded that they are not properly prepared for retirement. They feel afraid of retirement because they are not properly prepared for it. In the end, the key is in preparing properly for retirement.

Visitor : Therefore, the biggest reason why you feel anxious about retirement, as you suggest, is that we have not been adequately prepared for it. Is that correct?

Mentor: That's right. It's retirement preparation that cannot be emphasized enough. It's a message that retirement should not come to us as a fear like this. So, what would be a desirable way for retirement to come to us, instead of as fear?

Visitor : Well, I'm not sure if it's not fear!

Mentor: The way retirement comes to us, in my opinion, is through excitement. That's right. The real reason why retirement is feared is because of the lack of proper retirement preparation. If only retirement preparation is done properly, retirement can approach us not as fear, but as excitement. As I mentioned yesterday, starting with the preparation for a life that can be enjoyed alone called 'Sollive', preparing for a life enjoyed together called 'Comlive', preparing for a life of endless challenges and learning called 'Challive', and preparing for a life of enjoying while serving called 'Vollive', through these processes, one can create their own long-pursued field of interest, their 'Self-core brand'. This theory suggests that retirement preparation can be almost perfectly completed.

Visitor: I see. Now that I clearly understand the reasons why retirement is feared and know the countermeasures, there is no reason to be afraid of retirement anymore.

Mentor: That's right. Among the top five real reasons why people fear retirement, the absolute majority reason is the lack of proper retirement preparation. Therefore, if we prepare for retirement concretely in advance, it seems that we can eliminate our fear of retirement.

Visitor : Since I've visited here, it feels like the things that have been difficult for a while are gradually getting resolved one by one. However, how can I proceed with all these tasks? It seems like it would require a lot of time.

Mentor: Of course, it requires a lot of time. However, it's not about doing all these things at once, but about developing good habits and practicing a little bit every day. I believe that most successful people also build their success by developing good habits day by day.

Visitor : I agree. It seems that most successful people also believe in developing good habits to create their success. So, what are some good habits of successful people? I'm particularly interested to hear about the good habits you possess.

Mentor: I am not someone who has achieved great success, and I am currently in the process of learning and growing. Rather than calling them my habits, I have a set of principles that I have compiled by deeply reading certain books that moved me and incorporating them with my own life philosophy. I always strive to apply them in my daily life. To solidify them as definite habits, I write down keywords and constantly refine them through practice.

Adopt the 7 habits of successful people

Visitor : I find it incredibly fascinating that you have summarized the habits of successful people with keywords.

Mentor: At first, I became interested in habits and started researching in more detail what specific habits successful people have. This is because I realized that in order to succeed, it is important for us to understand the common habits of successful people and acquire them before it's too late. During this process, I came across a book that I consider as my bible, which is none other than 'The 7 Habits of Highly Effective People' by Stephen Covey. It is a widely known book that has been hailed as one of the best self-help books and continues to be loved as a work of humanities literature. I referred to this book and created my own set of 7 habits that I should emulate, assigning keywords to make them easier to understand and remember. I believe that recalling these keywords in everything I do will make it easier to put them into practice.

Visitor : I am deeply impressed by your constant effort to make anything good that you come across your own. So, what are the 7 keyword habits that you have summarized?

Mentor: To become a successful person, the 7 keyword habits we should have are 1. Tank habit, 2. Archery target habit, 3. Buffet plate habit, 4. Win-win habit, 5. Counselor habit, 6. Migratory birds habits, 7. Spring habit. I have assigned these habits. If you remember these 7 keywords, it seems that you can understand the core content sufficiently.

7 keywords of successful people's habits

Visitor : Then, please explain them one by one. The first one is the tank habit.

Mentor: Let me explain. The first habit among the 7 habits of successful people is the 'Tank Habit,' which means to take control of one's life like a tank. Imagine a tank charging steadfastly towards its goals. This first habit sends a message to take the lead in one's own life, just like a tank. It means that each individual must be the subject of their own life and take responsibility for it. You can interpret it as living a life where you are in charge of your own life and take responsibility for it.

Visitor: Living a self-directed life is precisely the tank habit. It resonates with me.

Mentor: That's right. If we blame others for what happens around us as we live our lives, we will be giving away the control of our own lives to others. It is about developing the habit of living a self-directed life, silently and steadfastly like a tank, without using others as an excuse. Always remember that you can only live a self-directed life if you never make excuses for others.

Visitor : I see. The first habit to have is living a self-directed life without making excuses to others. Then, what about the second one?

Mentor: The second habit among the seven habits of successful people is referred to as the 'Archery Target Habit'. When shooting an arrow in archery, what do we focus on? Don't we only pull the bowstring while looking at the final target? This means to start with the end in mind. In archery, we aim at the final target and consider all factors such as distance and wind strength to shoot towards the target. Just like the final target is important in archery, having a goal to strive for is important in our lives. Stephen Covey suggested planning everything by already considering how we will be remembered when our life comes to an end. He proposes writing something like a 'personal mission statement' as a specific method. Don't think too hard about it, but write down guidelines for the life you aspire to and refer to it in everything you do. That thing stuck to the wall above my desk is my personal mission statement. I have written down four aspects in it.

Visitor : I should write it as soon as I get home. The next, third habit is the 'Buffet plate Habit'. I'm really curious about how you incorporated the concept of a plate at a buffet.

Mentor: The third habit among the seven habits of successful people is the 'Buffet plate Habit', which means prioritizing what is important. When we go to a wedding buffet, we carefully select the food we want on an empty plate. In our lives, we should also carefully identify what is important to us and establish priorities for what we need to do first. If we approach a buffet with greed and put everything on our plate from the beginning, we may end up not being able to fully enjoy the truly delicious dishes. We can't waste what we've taken, we feel full, and we often regret it later, right? This is a reminder not to have such regrets in our lives.

Visitor : The message is to have a habit of prioritizing important things, just as we eat delicious food first when we go to a wedding buffet. It's a great analogy. What about the next habit?

Mentor: The fourth habit among the seven habits of successful people is called 'Win-win Habit', which means seeking mutual benefit. It encourages us to play a win-win game where both you and I win. In other words, it suggests that we should always strive to find solutions that satisfy not only ourselves but also the other party. In many cases, we have lived with the mindset of pursuing our own victory, just like in a football game. However, what if there is a way for both parties to achieve victory? Shouldn't we choose that path? This message is about creating a habit of making efforts to escape the paradigm of winning or losing and to generate mutually beneficial outcomes.

Visitor : This is indeed a habit that we can easily overlook. So, to remember the 'Win-win Habit', it can be seen as a habit of a win-win game where both you and I win. Next is the 'Counselor Habit'. What does it mean?

Mentor: The fifth habit among the seven habits of successful people is the 'Counselor Habit'. Its meaning is to first listen to the other person's perspective and then make them understand. This habit is an explanation of how to listen to others' stories with a more attentive attitude, empathize with them, and gain the ability to understand them. It is like saying, 'Let's create good habits like a good counselor'. A good counselor always listens to the other person's story first. Without fully listening to the other person's perspective, a counselor cannot provide accurate advice, right? Communication is ultimately about delivering messages between parties. You must listen carefully to the other person's story to clearly convey your message.

Visitor : I see. Indeed, listening carefully cannot be missing from good habits. It seems that being good at listening is one of the good habits of successful people. What is the next, the sixth one?

Mentor: The sixth of the seven habits of successful people is called the 'Migratory birds Habits'. However, this habit can also be referred to as the 'geese's V formation habit'. which emphasizes the power of synergy achieved by working together. Geese form a V-shaped flock and migrate together during winter. It is said that this allows them to travel about 71% faster than if they were flying individually. Synergy refers to the idea that the combined strength of a group is greater than the sum of its individual parts, resulting in better outcomes when people work together. So, how can we create such synergy? According to Stephen Covey, it is essential to acknowledge and respect our differences, while also complementing each other's weaknesses. If couples also acknowledge, respect, and complement each other's differences and weaknesses, they can build a relationship filled with synergy, don't you think?

Visitor: Even in a long-lasting marriage, if both partners acknowledge, respect, and complement each other's differences and weaknesses, it creates a synergistic effect. These words really resonate with me. Now, there is one last habit remaining. What is it?

Mentor: Oh, it's already the last one. The seventh habit of successful people is the 'Spring Habit' which means constantly renewing oneself. Steven Covey emphasized that to achieve ultimate success, one must constantly renew oneself through prayer, meditation, exercise and volunteerism, reading, and so on. This habit can ultimately be considered a habit of recharging, and can be a root habit for continuous self-improvement. There is a spring in the place where I exercise early in the morning that constantly flows fresh water. It is like understanding that one must always polish and renew their body and mind, just like the water from that spring, overflowing with freshness.

Visitor :   Now I understand exactly what you mean. It seems like the last habit should always be sharpened and polished like the water from a spring. All seven habits that you have provided so far seem to be really important habits for us.

Mentor: That's right. I also make an effort to cultivate these seven keywords as habits. I always incorporate these 7 habits, which I have summarized as keywords, when developing the 4 Areas of Retirement Preparation. 'Tank Habbit' is closely related to Sollive and is an essential habit when preparing for a self-directed life. 'Archery target Habit' and 'Buffet plate Habit' are closely related to Challive, indicating the need for habits that define clear goals and systematically develop them one by one when developing Challive items. 'Win-win Habit', 'Counselor Habit', and 'Migratory birds Habits' seem to align with the meaning of Comlive. The habit of preparing for a life of enjoying together should be used in developing items that satisfy each other and reflect the other person's perspective, creating synergy together. Lastly, the 'Spring Habit' signifies the habit of always renewing oneself and is closely related to Vollive. By remembering these 7 words - tank, archery, buffet, win-win, counselor, migratory birds, spring - I believe we can all have good habits to become successful individuals.

Visitor : You've provided a great explanation by turning the 7 habits of successful people into keywords and linking them to the 4 areas of retirement preparation. The emphasis becomes clear with the association of these 7 keywords. Live a self-directed life like a tank. Start by focusing on the target point, like shooting arrows after looking at the final target in archery. Start with the most important things, like filling an empty plate first at a buffet. Choose ways for you and me to win together as habits. Be a good counselor by listening carefully to the other person's words. Fly together like a flock of birds in a V-shape to create synergy. Always renew yourself like a spring in the early morning. Can I summarize your words like this?

Mentor: You summarized it really well. I must emphasize that your learning ability is truly outstanding.

Visitor : Thank you. I think all seven of them are good habits that should be cherished. However, like you mentioned, I also strive to challenge myself towards a goal, but I struggle when it comes to actually taking on the challenges. You mentioned a few times that there are special methods to approaching challenges. It seems like you have your own special challenge technique. I would appreciate it if you could provide a more detailed introduction to that method.

Mentor: Oh! You already caught on. There is a 4-stage rule of challenge to easily achieve your personal goals. If you follow this rule, you can easily achieve your challenged goals.

Visitor : As I expected, you have a secret method. Please share your wisdom.

Mentor: Take a moment to think. How many challenges have we overcome, big and small, to achieve our dreams up until now? Countless. Starting from the memory of my first challenge, where I ran for class president in elementary school and ended up with only three votes, to university entrance exams, employment, promotion, marriage, and even learning a musical instrument after retirement, our lives have been a series of challenges. However, these challenging processes have rarely felt easy. Some people seem to excel at everything they do, effortlessly achieving their goals, while I wonder why I'm struggling and feeling disappointed. Every challenge feels slow and even the thought of attempting something new becomes intimidating. We've all experienced this, wondering why things don't work out for us or why it feels so difficult. We complain and lose confidence, but it's not like anything gets easily resolved. So, what sets apart those challenge masters who seem to effortlessly succeed? Do they have their own secrets or techniques? This time, I would like to introduce the hidden rules that these challenge masters, who easily succeed in their goals, hold dear-the so-called WILD rule. I already explained the WILD rule yesterday. Do you remember?

Visitor : Ah, I remember. However, since it's an important part, I would appreciate it if you could summarize it once again. The WILD rule really resonates with me.

4 stages of the WILD rule

Mentor: Sure. I will briefly summarize it for you. WILD here can be said to be an acronym formed by combining the initials of Want, Imagine, Learn, and Declare.

Visitor : You said that WILD stands for Want, Imagine, Learn, and Declare, combining the first letters of each word. Is that correct?

Mentor: Sure! Let me explain each step. The first initial of WILD, W, stands for Want, which means to deeply desire your goal. The most significant characteristic of successful individuals in their endeavors is the intense desire and urgency for a particular goal. If you approach a goal with an attitude of 'I can do it if I want to, but it's okay if I don't, or even if I can't,' then that goal is already doomed from the start. To challenge anything, it is essential to have a strong desire for that goal as the first step. A strong sense of purpose and urgency act as the first button to make your challenges successful.

Visitor: To succeed in a challenge, it is necessary to deeply desire the goal. Does that fit your explanation?

Mentor: That's correct. It was mentioned that there is no greater motivation than intense desire. The second step of the four-step formula for successful challenges is represented by the letter I in WILD, which stands for Imagine. Yuval Noah Harari, the author of 'Sapiens,' a historian from Israel, once said, "Imagination made humans the protagonists of this planet". Additionally, William James, a psychologist from Harvard University in the United States, also stated, "Anything you can imagine, you can make real". Imagination is indeed a crucial weapon for achieving any challenging goal. If you wish to succeed in a challenge, you must imagine yourself achieving that goal. This is the best way to evoke autonomy, the ultimate factor of motivation.

Visitor : The advice is to imagine yourself achieving the goal. I think it is an essential step.

Mentor: Do you happen to know the British band Queen, which is considered the greatest vocalist in rock and pop music?

Visitor: Oh, I know. I listened to a lot of songs by the band Queen when I was in college. But why do you ask??

Mentor: Within the band Queen, there was a legendary vocalist named Freddie Mercury. He was originally an ordinary unknown singer with the real name Farrokh. During his unknown days, he always imagined himself singing on a big stage in front of thousands of people. He drew strength from such imagination, and it led to the creation of the famous masterpiece 'Bohemian Rhapsody'. It can be said that it is crucial for us to imagine the image of ourselves succeeding when embarking on any challenge.

Visitor: Imagination is really important. But does that mean everything will come true if we only imagine the image of ourselves succeeding?

Mentor: No, it's not. That's a big imagination. After that big imagination, you need to imagine the details. That detail imagination is imagining the methodology of how to achieve that goal.

Visitor : Do you mean imagining the methodology?

Mentor: Yes, that's right. It's imagining the specific methods or actions needed to achieve the goal. For example, in my case, if I set a goal to become a home chef and cook food for my family, in the initial stage of imagination, I envision myself cooking a steak and beautifully plating it, while my family enjoys the meal at the dining table and gives a thumbs-up while showing their approval. Then, in the second stage of detailed imagination, I would research and plan what I need to do and how to achieve this. In my case, I decided to pursue it professionally by obtaining a national certification. After attending a culinary academy for a few months, I obtained the certification, and now I enjoy the pleasure of cooking for my family as a home chef. Thus, this two-step detailed imagination of the methodology is very important.

Visitor : Thinking about how to achieve the goal is using detailed imagination. I understand. Then, what does 'L' stand for? Could it be 'Learn', meaning to acquire new knowledge or skills?

Mentor: Exactly. You have a great sense of understanding. It means learning in the direction that comes from detailed imagination. The third step of the 4-step success formula is represented by the third initial 'L' in the English acronym WILD, which stands for 'Learn'. It emphasizes passionate learning. This is the most crucial step that determines the success of the challenge, as it provides the specific actionable steps to achieve the goal. Nothing in this world happens overnight. The best approach is to practice little by little, according to the planned schedule, every day. It requires patience, as rushing or easily giving up is not an option. Just dreaming of playing a musical instrument won't make you a virtuoso overnight. We must clearly understand that those who have achieved their goals have gone through their own efforts and endured hardships over time.

Visitor : I will keep that in mind. So you're saying that all the goals we achieve are accomplished through learning. Then, what about the last step, the initial 'D' in WILD? I'm not quite sure what it means. I'd like to learn more about this particular aspect in greater detail.

Mentor: Let me explain. Among the four steps of the success formula, the last step is represented by the letter 'D' in the acronym WILD, which stands for Declare. It means making your challenge goals known to others, essentially declaring them. This step is also extremely important and can be seen as the hidden ultimate weapon of successful people. There are no specific rules on how to declare your goals; you can simply say them out loud or share them in a family band or group chat. However, it is highly recommended to make sure that your family and close ones are aware of your goals. This helps create a protective barrier that prevents your determination from easily crumbling.

Visitor : D stands for Declare, as you mentioned. It's important to make sure that close people around us are aware of our goals. Then, you mentioned yesterday that you use 'Practical bucket list' as your own declaration method, and it plays a crucial role in achieving your goals. I believe this aspect is highly significant. I'm truly sorry, but could you please summarize it once again? I would greatly appreciate it.

All roads to 'Practical bucket list'

Mentor: Great. Let me summarize my 'Practical bucket list' once again. It is indeed a crucial aspect. Think of my 'Practical bucket list' as the control tower that manages my goals, much like an air traffic control tower managing an airport runway. As I explain to you, I have been operating a 'Practical Bucket List' since my retirement, and it is attached to the wall in my private office. I highly recommend this method. Can you see it on the wall? That is my most cherished treasure. Through this method, I have pursued around 75 goals from retirement until now. Out of those, approximately 48 have been completed, and around 27 are still in progress. There will always be countless new items to challenge in the future. Do you know what the number one item on my 'Practical bucket list' is?

My Practical Bucket list

Visitor : Well, let me go and check it out once.

Mentor: Please go and have a look. You need to personally verify it once.

Visitor: It's 'Cooking 500 dishes for my wife until I die.' Wow! Making 500 dishes, that's not an easy challenge. Is it possible? How many have you done so far?

Mentor: So far, I have completed morn than 300 of it. I'm making steady progress to finish it successfully. It's true that my passion has somewhat cooled compared to the beginning, but I'm still steadily progressing. The biggest problem is that my wife's taste keeps getting higher. At first, she said all the food I made was delicious, but these days, her taste has become very picky.

Visitor : You're truly amazing. Looking at your 'Practical bucket list', you have a wide range of unique challenges.

Mentor: Within around 75 goals I have set so far, everything I want to do, things I want to challenge myself with, and things I must accomplish are all recorded. Many of the new titles I achieved after retirement can be seen as being conceived right here in this 'Practical bucket list', This is my incubator for challenges. It includes publishing a book related to retirement preparation and becoming an author, becoming a lecturer in various fields, becoming a songwriter, becoming an interviewer for public institutions, becoming a mentor for college students seeking employment interviews, obtaining more than 10 useful certifications, becoming a

YouTuber, playing the shoulder keyboard and drums, and so on. Everything started from this 'Practical bucket list', Even the recent publication of my poetry collection started from here. Soon, my new goals for challenges will also be recorded here, reaching out to the world. This 'Practical bucket list', is truly the most precious guiding light for me. It is the starting point for my challenges. Every time I start something from here, I always keep this phrase in mind: 'Challenges always pay off in the end.'

Visitor : 'Challenges always pay off in the end.' It's such a great saying. Everything is truly remarkable. After retirement, you were just like any regular retiree, but there were hidden reasons behind your transformation. After hearing your teachings on the WILD 4-step secret, it feels like I can take on any challenge. Please, once again, emphasize to make sure I don't forget.

Mentor: Ok, In summary, to challenge any goal, you need steps, which can be represented by the four-step secret of WILD, which is a method of succeeding in challenges. It can be summarized as: desire strongly, imagine vividly, learn fervently, and declare confidently. I am currently using this four-step secret and finding it very effective, so I recommend that anyone try it out for themselves. Don't worry too much about the future, just confidently challenge yourself according to the WILD. It really makes challenges easier.

Visitor: Got it. I'll make sure to put it into practice. However, you mentioned not to worry too much about the future. Actually, I tend to worry a lot about everything. Is there no way to overcome worries like that?

How to win against worries

Mentor: Best methods to alleviate worries! Yes, they exist. The method to overcome worries is very simple.

Visitor : You said the method is very simple?

Mentor: Yes, it is. To overcome worries, We must face our worries head-on and conquer them.

Visitor : You said we should face our worries head-on and conquer them. What do you mean?

Mentor: I'll teach you how to conquer your worries. Are you excited?

Visitor : Yes. I'm really looking forward to listening the way. Please tell me quickly.

Mentor: When we look around us, we can see many people who tend to worry excessively. People who believe in the saying 'Worry is also fate' accept worry as their destiny and live in a state of constant tension. Even if we tell them not to worry, it's not easy to change. Especially when it comes to health concerns, we often see cases where worries go beyond a reasonable level. One example is 'Doctor shopping.' These are people who, despite doctors reassuring them, continue to visit different doctors, convinced that they will soon find a new illness like shopping for new products at a department store. Now, I will share methods to alleviate these various worries. To do this, we need to challenge our worries. By facing them head-on and winning, we can make worries disappear. There are two stages to this approach.

Visitor : Did you mention that there are two stages of approach even when facing worries head-on? So what is the first stage?

2 stages to win against worries

1 Who are you? Are you a worry?	2 Hey, Worry! Let's have a showdown!

Mentor: The first stage is to question, "Who are you? Are you a real worry?" In other words, it suggests evaluating whether the current worry is truly worth worrying about. Generally, we tend to worry to prepare ourselves for impending difficulties and to wisely resolve matters that require our attention. If there were a case where one had sufficient reasons to worry, that worry would become a matter worthy of sufficient concern. However, most of our worries are futile. Canadian psychologist Ernie J. Zelinski described in his book 'The Joy of Not Knowing' that '40% of the worries we have will never happen in reality. 30% are about things that have already happened, and 22% are trivial matters that we need not be concerned about. Furthermore, 4% of worries are things we cannot change no matter how hard we try, leaving only 4% that we can actually change.' In essence, 96% of worries are either beyond our control or unnecessary.

Visitor : It means that we worry too much without reason, as only about 4% of our worries are actually worth worrying about.

Mentor: Yes, correct. In Tibetan proverb, there is a famous saying: 'If worrying could solve your problems, then there would be no worries left to worry about.' It means that worrying doesn't make your worries disappear. An American writer also compared worrying to a rocking chair. A rocking chair may rock you back and forth, but it doesn't take you anywhere. Worrying is similar in that it only makes us feel difficult and troubled without providing a fundamental solution. Therefore, it's important not to be too entangled in worries and take a step back to objectively assess if it's really worth worrying about. The answer to the first step of relieving worries, "Who are you? Are you a worry?", should

ideally be concluded as "Oh, I'm sorry. I'm not a worry".
Do you understand?

Visitor : Yes, I understand perfectly well. Since we're worrying too
much about unnecessary things, isn't it suggesting that we
first evaluate if the worries we currently have are truly
worth worrying about? Among the worries we have, it's
said that 96% of them are not worth worrying about. It's a
statement that resonates with me. So, what is the second
step?

Mentor: The second step in the approach to winning against
worries is "Hey, Worry! Let's have a showdown!" In other
words, it's an active approach to resolving worries
promptly when they are identified as worries. Based on
the 'Magic formula' to solve worries presented by
American writer Dale Carnegie, I propose an effective
method with three newly organized steps.

Visitor : There is a magic formula to solve worries? What are the
three steps in that process?

3 steps for resolving worries

Writing down	Listing down	Focusing

Mentor: The first step is to anticipate and write down the worst possible outcome when a worrying situation arises. Finding true inner peace comes from accepting the worst-case scenario. Next, the second step is to list down all the things I can do to address the assumed worst situation. Finally, in the third step, I determine what I am best equipped to do among the listed items and take immediate action.

Visitor : So, the essence of your statement is that the three-step formula for resolving worries is: first, writing down the worst possible outcome when we anticipate and worry about something, second, listing down all the things we can do to address the assumed worst situation. Finally, determining what we are best equipped to do among the listed items and taking immediate action.

Mentor: That's right. In other words, it's not time that solves the problem, but our own concrete efforts to solve the problem at hand. Interestingly, during this process, 50% of our worries disappear in the first step, and 40% of our worries can be resolved in the second step, leaving only 10% of our worries behind. Ultimately, if we focus intensively on solving the remaining 10%, it can greatly help us in resolving our worries.

Visitor: So, what you're saying is that we often engage in unnecessary worries, but instead of doing that, we should minimize our concerns and directly confront the real issues. By doing this, our focus will improve, making it easier for us to resolve them more effectively. Is that an accurate summary?

Mentor: Got it. This simple approach really does have an impact. You should definitely try it out sometime. The second step in this method of resolving worries concludes with the response to the worry of "Hey worry, let's fight!" being "Oh no, I've lost. I will now disappear."

Visitor : Your fun and engaging way of expressing it really helped me understand it better.

Mentor: Thank you for understanding well. In the process of living our lives, it's impossible to not have worries. However, we shouldn't waste our life's energy on unnecessary worries. Just worrying doesn't make things better at all. Unnecessary worries only lead to more worries. Therefore, I recommend that you try to solve any worries you have by using the method I suggested, especially for the things that are causing you to worry.

Visitor : I will definitely keep that in mind. It seems like more than half of my worries have already disappeared. You seem to be able to analyze any problem, find solutions, and successfully apply them as your own. How is that possible?

Mentor: The key to the solution lies in note-taking. I mentioned the importance of note-taking and record-keeping before. Let me show you the evidence right now.

He stood up from his seat and walked towards the desk, bringing along about ten different notebooks and a bundle of around a thousand cards. The notebooks had 'Storytelling Note 1, 2, 3...' written on their covers, and there was something meticulously written inside. Each notebook had summarized content categorized by topic, with the date of writing, sources, subjects, authors, and more. The visitor could only imagine how much time it must have taken him to organize such a vast amount of information. He explained to the visitor that after retiring, he summarized all the valuable content from books, magazines, articles, lectures, TV, YouTube, and more. Then, what's more surprising is that the bundle of around a thousand cards. The bundle was divided into about ten sets, and each set was labeled 'Storytelling Cards' on the front. Each individual card was densely filled with content related to a different theme. The visitor now had a rough idea of where his expertise came from.

Visitor : You are truly amazing. You read, watch, and listen to everything and organize it all so meticulously. I think I understand why you emphasize the importance of note-taking. But what does 'Storytelling note and card' mean on the cover?

Mentor: A 'Storytelling note and card' is a notebook and card where I summarize all the information in a concise and storytelling manner. The reason I started writing these notes and cards is that whenever I give lectures, I want to introduce valuable content from books, but if it's not well-organized, it becomes difficult to convey. That's why I pre-organize the information I read, watch, and listen to into these notes and cards, categorized by topic, to make it easier for me to give short storytelling during the lectures. For example, if there is a topic on 'imagination', I can easily find relevant information in my notes, which greatly helps in preparing materials. Sometimes, it takes more time to organize than actually reading the books. It's not an easy task, but I find it incredibly rewarding.

Visitor : I see. Storytelling notes and cards! I should give it a try too. But it must be difficult to find time for hobbies when you spend so much time on this, isn't it?

Mentor: Hobby activities? Of course, they are also so important. Let's have a conversation about hobbies this time. What hobby do you currently have?

Hobbies should be like clothes

Visitor : I don't have a specific hobby planned for after retirement yet. I'm considering trying to play a musical instrument.

However, I'm not sure what to pursue yet.

Mentor: It might not be easy for you to make decisions when it comes to what you want to do. That's why it's important not to just choose any hobby after retirement. You need to choose a hobby that suits you. Choosing the wrong hobby after retirement can actually be detrimental.

Visitor : It could be detrimental, you said That makes it even more difficult to choose.

Mentor: That's why this time, I'm thinking of offering four tips on how to create a hobby that suits you.

Visitor : Four tips on how to create a hobby that suits me? That would be really helpful. This topic is also very interesting to me.

Mentor: In today's era of living up to 100 years, we all know that hobbies are being highlighted as an essential requirement for an active retirement, don't we? According to internet data, 74% of retirees responded that hobby activities are very important in life. This means that hobbies are now considered as important for retirement as financial planning. Especially considering that these hobbies play a significant role in forming new social connections in old age, their significance becomes even greater. However, if we simply dive into any hobby after retirement without careful consideration, it can actually become detrimental. It's like wearing clothes that don't suit us. Many people start something just because others are doing it, only to find themselves unsatisfied. In such cases, it ultimately leads to wasting money, time, and even losing passion, to the point where they may not even have the courage to try something new. That's why, based on my personal experience, I want to provide some tips on creating hobbies that are suitable for oneself, in order to avoid the pitfalls of making wrong choices and make our retirement fantastic.

Visitor: Based on your real-life experience, this becomes even more fascinating. Please break it down step by step.

Mentor: One of the four tips for creating a hobby that suits me is to choose a hobby that can be enjoyed alone and occasionally shared with others. In old age, hobbies are an important area that allows you to spend time alone while connecting with social life. Therefore, as a principle to consider when choosing such hobbies, I recommend 'together yet separate'.

4 tips for creating hobbies

Together yet separate	Start small	Challenge a long-buried dream	Productive & shareable

Visitor : 'Together yet separate'? What does that mean?

Mentor: This principle means choosing a hobby that can be easily enjoyed alone as well as shared with others. By following this principle, not only can we increase the fun and fulfillment, but it can also have a significant impact on self-satisfaction and forming new relationships. Such hobbies can become a presence like vitamins, rather than being isolating or detrimental. Let me give you an example from my wife's case.

Visitor : Sure, that sounds great.

Mentor: My wife, who never had a hobby before, started learning how to play the ukulele one day. She practices and enjoys it alone at home on regular days, but once a week, she joins others for group practice. And whenever there's an opportunity, she even participates in joint performances with club members. It's truly delightful to see. This is a great example of 'together yet separate.' There are countless activities that can be pursued as hobbies, even if it's not playing a musical instrument.

Visitor : I see. It seems like the 'together yet separate' principle is important. So, what is the second tip?

Mentor: The second tip out of the four tips for creating a hobby that suits me is to not start too grandly, but to start with something small and easy. It means that there's no need to prefer something grand and expensive. It's about the curiosity that you can temporarily be interested in a specific activity. For example, I've seen cases where someone was fascinated by camper vans during their retirement motivation and spent a lot of money to buy one, but after using it a few times, he realized it didn't suit him and ended up regretting it for years. It's important not to rush from the beginning and to start with small hobbies that you can easily do. If someone wants to learn the guitar, they can simply buy a used guitar from a second-hand market and participate in a community center program to start. If someone loves poetry and wants to publish a poetry book, they should start by writing at least one poem now. If you don't start right away, you won't achieve anything.

Visitor : So the advice is to start small and steadily, without rushing. What about your case?

Mentor: I also started with something small that I could easily do. In my case, my hobby is writing. One day, after retiring, I wanted to give my wife a poem as a thank you gift for all the support she had given me. The poem was titled 'My Wife Inside of Me', and it ended up becoming a song that I recorded. From there, I started writing more songs and eventually debuted as a songwriter. It's really important to start. If I hadn't started writing that poem for my wife that night, I wouldn't have been able to experience the birth of

'Gyeongju Arirang', which is now the representative song of Gyeongju. Starting is everything. It's really important.

Visitor: I really relate to the importance of starting small. It hits close to home. So what's the third tip?

Mentor: The third tip out of four for finding a hobby that suits me is to challenge myself with a hobby that fulfills my long-buried dreams. Everyone may have one or two dreams they've always wanted to pursue since their youth. How about trying to challenge those dreams that seem impossible? Dreams were just dreams if we never touch them. Dreams become reality only when we take action. I've seen people in their 60s who, after postponing it for a long time, mustered the courage to learn swimming and became children's swimming instructors after retirement. Isn't that amazing?

Visitor : So, have you also challenged that kind of dream you've put aside?

My oldest dream is 'Venus'

Mentor: Of course, I also challenged that dream. My oldest dream dates back to my middle school days when I was captivated by someone playing pop songs on the drums and I dreamt of learning to play the drums myself someday. The song that really got me hooked was 'Venus' by Shocking Blue. I never gave up on that dream for 40 years. It's only now, after 40 years, that I finally extended my challenge to play drums. So I started learning the drums, and I've already completed over 30 out of my goal of 33 songs. There's a saying that I always emphasize when I give lectures: 'If you have a dream, never throw it in the trash can. Because dreams hate trash cans the most.'

Visitor: 'Dreams hate trash cans the most.' That's such a cool saying. I also wanted to learn to play drums. It's really amazing that you've played over 30 songs. Which songs have you played?

Mentor: I have loved pop songs since I was young, and I practice a lot of fast-paced songs among them. For example, old pop songs like Venus, Bad Case of Loving You, Brother Louie, Stumblin' In, Sunny, Wanted, and Stayin' Alive. It's truly an exciting challenge.

Visitor : That's really impressive. Then, can we take a short break here and listen to one drum song? That room over there is the music room, right? I caught a glimpse of it earlier.

Mentor: Sure, shall I play one drum performance for you and then we can continue?

He guided the visitor to the music room. At the entrance of the door, there was a sign that said 'Present Room/Amusement'. As soon as the door opened, the visitor was completely amazed. It was not a large room, but a drum set was placed at the edge, neatly accompanied by a shoulder keyboard and a guitar. On the opposite side, there was an accordion, flutes, and harmonicas were also visible. It was a complete music room itself.

Visitor : You have quite a collection of instruments. Do you play all of these instruments?

Mentor: No, I mainly play the drum and the shoulder keyboard. I practice the Janggu and the accordion occasionally.

Visitor : This instrument is new to me. It looks like a guitar and also like a keyboard, doesn't it?

Mentor: Yes, that's right. That's why it's called a 'shoulder keyboard' because you wear it on your shoulder. It's also sometimes called a 'keytar' because it can be played like a guitar. It has keyboard functionality, allowing you to produce the sounds of many instruments.

Visitor : Do you practice this instrument as well?

The reason to practice shoulder keyboard

Mentor: Yes, I have selected 10 songs and I'm practicing them repeatedly with this shoulder keyboard. I'm planning a small family music concert for my wife's 60th birthday anniversary.

Visitor : So, you're practicing 10 songs and planning a small family concert for your wife? That's wonderful! What songs are included in the 10 songs?

Mentor: There are 3 pop songs and 7 Korean songs. For example, the pop songs are 'For the Good Times', 'Casablanca', and 'I Have a Dream'. As for the Korean songs, I focused on the ones that my wife likes. I have to practice hard because if I make even a small mistake on the keyboard, it will become a complete mess. OK, I will now attempt to play one song on the drum and one song on the shoulder keyboard, even though I still have a lot to improve.

Once he took his seat behind the drums, he began playing 'She's Gone' by Steelheart, a 5-member heavy metal band from the United States, a song he had been practicing recently. Even though he wasn't a professional, to the ears of the visitor, it sounded like a piece of art. Then, he proceeded to play the shoulder keyboard and started singing the song 'Casablanca', which was his wife's favorite. It was amazing to see him cultivate his hobby so splendidly after several years of being unable to do so. In the hearts of the visitor, there was a strong belief that he was undoubtedly a 'creator' who could forge his own path in life.

Visitor : I really enjoyed it. You did a great job. You're truly a professional, not just a title. You've written about all the experiences, experiments, and challenges you've gone through in a book, and you even give lectures. I'm totally impressed. By the way, how long did it take for you to learn these instruments?

Mentor: It didn't take long. I started after retiring from everything else. I've been playing the shoulder keyboard for about 3 years, and drums for around 2 years. I just dedicate a little bit of time and enjoy it. You should never try to master an instrument. It only builds up stress. Enjoying the process is very important for a hobby in retirement.

Visitor : I see. Enjoying the process is indeed crucial. So, what's the last and final tip related to creating a hobby?

Mentor: The fourth and final tip among the four tips for creating a hobby that suits you is to choose a hobby that is preferably productive and can be shared with others. As you know, personal inclination is crucial when it comes to hobbies. However, I recommend selecting a hobby that is not only personally fulfilling but also productive and shareable with others. Such hobbies will provide even more satisfaction as you grow older.

Visitor : So, the last tip is to choose a hobby that is productive and shareable with others. Can you please provide an example in your case?

Mentor: If I explain my own case, it might be easier for you to understand. After retiring, I pondered over what to do and ended up choosing cooking and baking. I attended cooking schools and obtained national certifications, and now I am enjoying my satisfying hobby. As I mentioned before, my number one item on my bucket list is the 'Cooking 500 dishes for my wife until I die' project. I have reached a turning point now. And I have set up a bread-making room to pursue home baking, and I occasionally bake bread at home. However, I am already curious about how it will feel to make warm milk bread or sausage bread for my soon-to-be-born granddaughter or grandson in the near future. This is an example of how a productive and altruistic hobby can bring fulfillment and continue to grow.

Visitor : That's impressive that you make bread at home. Where do you make it?

My home bakery 'Kilimanjaro'

Mentor: That small room on the right is the 'Future Room'. That's my home bakery room. I've named it 'Home Bakery Kilimanjaro'.

Visitor : Wow! You've even set up a room for baking bread. Home Bakery Kilimanjaro! It's such a cool name. Could you show me around?

The visitor couldn't help but be amazed as he entered the 'Creation Room'. It seemed that all the equipment was fully prepared. On one side, there was a sturdy metal table for bread-making, and on the adjacent table, they could see a dough mixer and an oven. On another side, various tools for baking, including flour and different ingredients, were neatly arranged. Recipes of some kinds were attached to A4 papers on the wall, and the sight of clean baking gowns hanging on a coat rack made a strong impression on the visitor. The visitor couldn't help but be amazed once again at how everything was concrete and practical. The thought that what he emphasized as 'concrete' meant exactly this struck the visitor deeply.

Visitor : So, what kind of bread do you mainly make here?

Mentor: I make various types of bread. From French bread called baguette, to Danish pastries, pies, cookies, and cakes. I make whatever I feel like making at the time.

Visitor : What kind of bread do you excel at making at home?

Mentor: Instead of saying that I make it well, I have a bread that I usually make on special occasions. It's called 'Stollen', which is mainly eaten during the German Christmas season. It's a premium bread that contains a lot of ingredients. It includes about 20 different ingredients, including white wine. I enjoy making this bread the most.

Visitor : I've never heard of that bread before. It sounds interesting, especially with wine in it. I'd love to try it sometime.

Mentor: If there's a chance next time, I'll make it for you. Actually, making bread is a great hobby to everyone, but there's one inconvenient thing. It takes a lot of time because there's a fermentation process in the middle. So when I make bread, I set aside a specific day to do it.

Visitor : Anyway, it seems like you approach your hobbies very systematically and professionally. There's so much to do to prepare for the second half of our life. I'm starting to feel anxious about retiring soon and becoming increasingly useless. I guess I need to change this mindset first.

Mentor: Exactly. It's a really important issue. As you get older, there are three types of thoughts that you shouldn't have, and among them, the most detrimental one is thinking that I've become useless now.

Visitor : You mentioned that there are three types of thoughts that we shouldn't have as we get older. Could you explain a bit more about what those three are?

Unhealthy thoughts while aging

Mentor: Let me explain. I think there are three types of thoughts that should not be had as you get older. The first one is the idea that 'I am now useless!' Among the various motivations that can move people in this world, love and fear are the most representative. However, as people approach death, many emotions tend to disappear or weaken, but these two emotions remain until the end. Among them, as you get older, fear looms larger than love. Fear comes to us in many forms, such as fear of inadequacy, fear of rejection, fear of not achieving anything, fear of becoming poor, fear of being alone, fear of not being acknowledged, and so on. Among them, the fear that you should never have as you get older is the fear that you are useless. If a word can kill a person in one word, then this phrase becomes a word that kills me.

3 types of unhealthy thoughts while aging

Visitor : Why is that?

Mentor: The reason is simple. This thought can immediately drain all the passion and energy I have and plunge me into a deep well of despair. Other people seem to continue living a meaningful life even after retirement, showing that they are constantly challenging themselves. They find new jobs, climb the Himalayas, learn musical instruments diligently, and seem to be living their lives to the fullest. But I'm just constantly worrying about what I should do, how I should live, and in the end, I become overwhelmed and think, 'I'm still not good enough! I have no value! I'm useless!' If I keep having these thoughts, it's like falling into a self-destructive path. What's truly useless is not me, but the fear of thinking that I am truly useless.

Visitor: I really understood. I will also strive to become a more useful person in my life. Now, I also want to hear two other things right now

Mentor: As you age, one of the three thoughts that you really shouldn't have is 'I really don't have time anymore!' But, is time really running out? Even if you retire, you still have plenty of time ahead, at least 30 years. That time is purely your own, unlike the past. It is ample time to prepare and fulfill your dreams. The key is how you utilize that time, isn't it?

Visitor : That's right. I completely agree with that point. So, what is the last thing?

Mentor: As you age, one of the three thoughts that you really shouldn't have is 'I really have nothing left!' It seems that it's not because you don't have anything, but rather because you haven't found satisfaction yet. Satisfaction is when you stop when the water reaches your ankles. What would happen if the water rose past your ankles, up to your waist, and even to the top of your head? It would be a big problem. That's why it shouldn't overflow. As you age, it seems that it's important not to have an excess or overflow of things.

Visitor : Then, the three things that you really shouldn't have as you age are 'I am useless, I don't have time, and I don't have anything.' I will remember that well. If I live my life as you advised during this 1 night and 2 days, my second act of life will be a very cool life.

Mentor: That's right. As we age, we should live more stylishly.

Visitor : Then do you have a solution for how we can live a stylish life?

Mentor: I think there are key points that people who live stylishly have, rather than a solution. So, let me unpack those contents for you.

Visitor: You really are like a wizard who easily explains the guidelines for life. I'm looking forward to more new content.

Four key traits of stylish people

Mentor: Then, what are the characteristics of people who live stylishly? I would like to summarize those characteristics into four.

Visitor : So, what is the first characteristic?

Mentor: The first of the four characteristics of stylish individuals is not postponing challenges in their lives anymore. Challenges are not exclusive to young people. Nowadays, we use the term 'Active seniors'. Typically, active seniors show characteristics of being active and enthusiastic, having the time and financial freedom after retirement. We also refer to them as 'Yolds,' a combination of 'Young' and 'Old.' However, the most significant characteristic of this Yold generation is their enjoyment of challenges, just like young people. Here, challenge refers to presenting themselves with opportunities they once dreamed of or things they have put off for a long time. Examples include seniors in their 60s who become models, learn to fly drones and travel around the country capturing videos, or those who learn musical instruments and perform busking despite having no prior background in music. They actively present themselves with challenges in various fields of society. Aren't they all truly amazing? But the key point is that these challenges are no longer things to be postponed. If you haven't presented yourself with a challenge for something you want to do yet, don't delay it any longer. It's time to take on the challenge now.

4 key traits of stylish people

Take on challenges	Embrace aging	Open mindedness	Action-oriented

Visitor : OK. The first characteristic of stylish people is that they enjoy challenges. So, what is the second characteristic?

Mentor: The second characteristic of stylish people who live stylishly is that they don't fear getting older and live confidently. No one can stop the passing of time. It may be a very sad thing. However, if you find the positive aspects of getting older and make good use of them, you can enjoy a more abundant life even as you age. Professor Howard Gardner of Harvard Medical School in the United States said that humans have 8 intelligences: logical-mathematical intelligence, spatial intelligence, bodily-kinesthetic intelligence, linguistic intelligence, musical intelligence, interpersonal intelligence, intrapersonal intelligence, and naturalistic intelligence. But the important thing is that among them, there is an intelligence that increases as you get older. Don't be surprised. Five out of the total eight intelligences have higher intelligence scores as you get older. Do you know which five they are?

Visitor : Naturalistic intelligence and intrapersonal intelligence are definitely going to be included.

Mentor: Yes, they will be included. The five intelligences mentioned are linguistic intelligence, musical intelligence, interpersonal intelligence, naturalistic intelligence, and intrapersonal intelligence. Many intelligences actually strengthen as we age. Have you happened to watch the movie 'The Intern', starring the legendary American actor Robert De Niro?

Visitor : I didn't see it in the theaters, but I think I watched it on Netflix.

Mentor: I watched it on Netflix too. I really enjoyed it. The movie leaves the deepest impression on us with the fact that the CEO, who leads a team of a whopping 220 people, is a young woman in her 30s, while the character who appears as an intern in the company is an elderly man in his 70s. Although he is an intern, this elderly man excels in the company's work with the wisdom, life experience, and sense he has accumulated over the years. Isn't it a good movie with such a story? But this is not just a story in the movie. I think if we live our lives without fearing aging, our lives can become more stylish and fulfilling.

Visitor : Even though we watched the same movie, you seem to see something special in it. So, what about the third one then?

Mentor: The third characteristic of people who live stylishly is to open their hearts, knowledge, and wallets. As you grow older, you should open your heart first. If there is any baggage in your heart, you should let it all out and open your heart wide. That way, you will feel more at ease. The next thing you should open is your knowledge. You should generously share the know-how and experiences you have accumulated in various fields with your juniors and local community. If you share your own experiences and knowledge through talent donation or volunteer activities, how stylish would your life be? Lastly, there is something that must be opened: your wallet. Depending on your situation and position, you should never be stingy when it comes to opening your wallet.

Visitor: So, you're saying that we should open our hearts, knowledge, and wallets. That's truly inspiring. What about the fourth one?

Mentor: The fourth and final characteristic of people who live stylishly is a very important one. It is to lead life through actions rather than just words. Richard Wiseman, a British psychologist and author of '59 Seconds: Think a Little, Change a Lot', said that when people's thoughts change, their actions change. The problem is that changing one's thoughts is not easy. Therefore, he advised that instead of trying to change your thoughts, change your actions first. By changing your actions, your thoughts will also change. This means that through small positive changes in behavior, you can develop good habits. This can be considered an essential element shared by successful people.

Visitor : So, it means that since it's difficult to change actions through thoughts, it's better to change thoughts through actions, and by continuously doing this, it can become a good habit.

Mentor: That's right. Among the sayings I like, there is one that goes, 'Thinking is not doing.' It means that we can't accomplish everything just by thinking. The concept of starting only counts when we take action, not just by thinking alone.

Visitor : I see. You really seem to always focus on action and implementation. I admire that. So, if we follow the four principles you mentioned, we can lead a cool and wonderful life, right? Could you summarize the key points once again?

Mentor: Of course, it's definitely possible. By consistently following those principles, we gradually develop into such individuals. To summarize the 4 characteristics of people who live stylishly: First, don't procrastinate challenges in your own life. Second, don't fear aging and live confidently. Third, open your heart, expand your knowledge, and be open with your wallet. Fourth, lead your life through actions rather than just words. That's how it can be summarized. All four are precious to me. I make daily efforts to live up to them little by little.

Visitor : It's really valuable advice. You've shared various practical methods, starting from how to prepare for retirement for 1 night and 2 days from different perspectives. It's all precious advice that I don't want to miss. I now have the courage to put it into practice. However, it seems that all these practices ultimately depend on how well we prepare in the 4 areas of retirement preparation.

Mentor: You've understood it correctly. The core of my book is exactly how to prepare well in the 4 areas of retirement preparation. If you look at what I have accomplished since my retirement, how many things have I done? It's like a dream come true. But those things were not even on my mind before retirement. Everyone has built them one by one based on the foundation of the 4 areas of retirement preparation. That's why I strongly recommend starting with the 4 areas of retirement preparation. By preparing in this way, your life in old age will be balanced, and you won't be looked down upon by anyone.

Visitor : You mean we won't be looked down upon even in old

age?

Mentor: That's correct. To avoid being disregarded even in old age, it is important to have a balanced life after retirement. It's not just about having a lot of money, but rather how well you prepare and maintain four areas of life with dignity. That is the key to guaranteeing the quality of life. That's why I emphasize the four areas of retirement preparation: Sollive, Comlive, Challive, and Vollive.

Visitor : Now I understand why you emphasize the 4 areas of retirement preparation, Sollive, Comlive, Challive, and Vollive. It means that by building these four areas well, we can have a strong life in our old age, be recognized and respected without being disregarded by others. So, could you please summarize the four areas of retirement preparation, Sollive, Comlive, Challive, and Vollive, in one final comprehensive way based on the content of your lectures so far? Would that be possible?

Succeeding as a retiree after retirement

Mentor: If it helps, I'll be more than happy to assist. I will summarize my story about the preparation process after retirement once again. After working for 35 years, as my retirement date approached, I became overwhelmed with anxiety about how to spend my retired life. I couldn't figure out what to do for retirement preparation, even though it was only 1 or 2 years away. I started to worry that I would become an unemployed person with no occupation, and to overcome these fears, I began reading retirement-related books in earnest to prepare myself for something. So, I purchased retirement books available in the market, about 20 out of the 40 books that I found online, and diligently read them. However, I couldn't find any specific guidelines on how retirees should prepare for retirement in any of those books.

Visitor : So, you couldn't find it in any of those books?

Mentor: Actually, I couldn't find it. I was so frustrated. So, I actively participated in retirement preparation programs provided by the company, consulted retiring seniors, and even sought advice from retirement experts, but I couldn't find any solution that offered practical and specific methods for retirement preparation. So, I became even more frustrated. I eventually thought that we couldn't properly prepare for retirement in Korea. I was curious about how other countries handle it, so I searched the internet and looked for books, but I couldn't find the answers I was looking for. That's when I started to sink deeper into my worries and eventually decided to create my own solution. After going through various trials and errors for about 2 years, I wrote the first practical retirement guidebook based on the results I had created. That's the book titled 'Eun-jun-in(Retirement preparer)'.

Vistor : Okay, got it. There's a proverb that goes, 'Necessity is the mother of invention', which fits perfectly in this situation. Keep talking, please.

Mentor: Yes, so the core of that book emphasizes the need to prepare for retirement, which everyone will eventually face, by focusing on four key areas of preparation. Through this, we should strive to achieve a balanced post-retirement life and develop a core that allows us to pursue and further develop the areas we are most passionate about, which can be sustained as a lifelong career. I refer to this as the 'Self-core brand'. However, for this 'Self-core brand' to be created, it is crucial that these '4 areas of retirement preparation' are solidly established. Only then can our lives achieve balance, and there will be no more instances of being disregarded just because we have grown older. The 4 areas of retirement preparation is more necessary than anything else.

Visitor : You mentioned that it is necessary to first achieve balance in life through the 4 areas of retirement preparation. Could you please summarize these 4 areas of retirement preparation for me?

Mentor: If I were to summarize the preparation process for the first stage, which is 'Sollive', it is the specific preparation for a life that can be enjoyed alone. This preparation is considered as the foundation for a wonderful retirement. I emphasized three things in this field. First, it is important to secure a living space that can be used for commuting. Second, it is necessary to secure a fixed living expense that can be used. Third, it is important to prepare things to enjoy alone, such as musical instruments, calligraphy, drawing, plant cultivation, cooking, etc. The second of the four key areas is the preparation for 'Comlive'. This preparation is to prepare concretely for a life that can be enjoyed together with those who will be closest to us after retirement, such as our spouse, family, and friends. The third is the preparation for 'Challive'. This preparation is to thoroughly prepare for a life of endless challenges and learning even after retirement, which is the field most likely to be connected to a lifelong occupation later on. In this field, I emphasized five things, starting from the challenge of a new language after retirement, acquiring certifications, actively participating in SNS operation such as YouTube and Naver blogs that suit each person's style, challenging the dream job for a long time, and expanding into other areas when one goal is achieved. Finally, the fourth is the preparation for 'Vollive'. This preparation is to thoroughly prepare for a life of enjoying volunteering even after retirement. I am emphasizing three points here. The first is that the starting point for volunteering after retirement is family. The second is that there are various ways of volunteering with talents, so use your own talents well. Lastly, it is important to participate in volunteer activities in the local community on a regular and continuous basis. Through this process of cultivating the 4 areas of retirement preparation, we can create a field that is of the greatest interest to us. If we specialize in it further, that will become our 'Self-core brand' that we aim for in the future. That will be our second career.

Visitor : Until now, You summarized the 4 Areas of Retirement Preparation and Self-core brand very well. Now I fully understand your teachings. I will follow what you have taught me and work hard to prepare for retirement.

Mentor: That's right. I firmly believe that if anyone is well-prepared in these 4 areas, our old age will be brighter than anyone else's. The reason is that I am doing it right now. Before retirement, I didn't have any plans at all, but through this ordinary method, I challenged myself step by step. Now, after retirement, I currently hold various titles such as a writer, instructor in multiple fields, lyricist, interviewer, job mentor, and YouTuber. Recently, I published a poetry collection called 'Life Shorts' for my wife. Now, I am truly satisfied with my life. I am confident that anyone can succeed in retirement life if they do it like this. I encourage you to challenge yourself. 'Challenges always lead to something worthwhile.'

Visitor : Thank you. I will definitely give it a try. Your words, filled with practical experiences over a long period of time, are truly moving. I will put them into practice for sure.

Mentor: Please become a successful retirement preparer. Thank you for listening attentively for a long time. I hope you have a safe journey to your next destination.

As the lectures for the '1 Night 2 Days' program came to an end, they stepped outside to bid farewell, only to find the night already embracing their surroundings. Despite the chilly breeze, a comforting warmth lingered between them. They held hands tightly, silently communicating their thoughts. When one smiled, the other mirrored the expression. The signboards of the quaint taverns and restaurants in the alley flickered together, as if touched by the bittersweet parting of the two.

Succeeding as a Retiree :
How to Prepare for Your Second Career